Johannes Grotzky
Chernobyl
The Catastrophe

Johannes GROTZKY (*1949)

Studied Slavonic and Balkan languages, History of Eastern and Southeastern Europe in Munich and Zagreb. 1983-1994 Correspondent in Moscow and Vienna (for Southeast Europe). 2002-2014 Radio Director of the Bavarian Broadcast Corporation (BR) in Munich. Honorary Professor for Eastern European Studies, Culture and Media at the University of Bamberg.

Johannes Grotzky

CHERNOBYL
The Catastrophe

Contemporary Reports
Commentaries
Inside Views

BoD

Bibliographical Information of the German National Library:
The German National Library lists this publication in the *Deutsche Nationalbibliografie*; detailed bibliographical data can be found on the Internet at http://dnb.d-nb.de

Production and publisher: BoD - Books on Demand GmbH, Norderstedt
ISBN 978-3-75260-811-3
Printed in Germany

WHY THIS BOOK?

The international book market is inundated with publications dealing with the disaster of the Soviet nuclear power plant of Chernobyl in 1986.

The Hollis catalogue of the Harvard Library – which includes 79 libraries – is one of the largest book collections in the world with a stock of 16.8 million volumes. This catalogue lists almost 118,480 publications[1] on the Chernobyl disaster.

These publications are of all media types (books, journal articles, dissertations, online-based materials, videos, conference papers, lectures) in more than 40 languages, including Russian. In addition to these publications there are another 5,608 titles under the Ukrainian name "Chornobyl".[2] Basically, every conceivable aspect of the disaster is discussed from every angle. Almost all the facts are known with a few exceptions.[3] The people responsible for the disaster are named and held accountable. The victims who lost their lives as a result of this catastrophe and those who will suffer the consequences of the contamination all their lives have

---

[1] Retrieved August 4, 2019 under https://hollis.harvard.edu/primo-explore/search?query=any,contains,Chernobyl&tab=everything&search scope=everything&vid=HVD2

[2] Retrieved August 4, 2019 under https://hollis.harvard.edu/primo-explore/search?query=any,contains,Chornobyl&tab=everything&search scope=everything&vid=HVD2&offset=0

[3] It is still unclear today what contaminated material is really located under the ruins of the fourth reactor , which is sealed as a sarcophagus, what long-term effects this will have, and how future generations will be able to handle this dangerous radioactive heritage.

received public sympathy. But no one can undo the terrible damage to life and limb.

So, why am I presenting this little volume on Chernobyl now when everything that matters has been published? Everything that was published after the Chernobyl catastrophe could refer to a lot of information and knowledge in retrospect. Here, the same rule applies as to war reporting. Real reporting only takes place after the end of the war, when all sources are accessible and all sides have been heard. But as in every war, there was also live reporting during the Chernobyl catastrophe, not knowing what happened in detail. This reporting was partly characterized by ignorance, a lack of information and the undermining of information, by speculations, fears and rumors. And that is exactly what this book is about.

As a correspondent in Moscow from 1983 to 1989 I was able to experience the agony under the ailing Secretary-Generals Andropov and Chernenko as well as the start of a risky reform policy under Mikhail Gorbachev. After taking office in March 1985, Gorbachev in particular attempted to develop the Soviet Union into a competitive model vis-à-vis the Western world by demanding more openness (*glasnost*) and a restructuring of the economy and society (*perestroika*).

The Chernobyl catastrophe occurred during the opening process of this reform policy – at the end of his first year in office. In spite of the new openness, we correspondents in Moscow – as well as the entire world – learned for almost two days nothing about the disaster in the fourth reactor unit of Chernobyl, taking place in the night from April 25-26, 1986. In West European countries increasing radioactivity had been measured already. It clearly came from the Soviet Union. Radio stations from Germany called me in Moscow and wanted to know more. I remember my first reaction when I said: If this was really a radioactive explosion within the Soviet

Union, then Gorbachev would be the first to go public because of his policy of *glasnost*.

But nothing happened and therefore we correspondents had nothing to report. Only two days later, on April 28, 1986 at 21:02 (9:02 p.m.) Moscow time, the Soviet news agency TASS[4] published in the Russian and English service an identical message consisting of four short sentences:

- An accident at the Chernobyl nuclear power plant was admitted, during which a reactor had been damaged.
- Measures had been taken to eliminate the consequences of the accident.
- Help had been given to those affected.
- A government commission had been set up.

The documentary part of this book begins with this TASS report. Further on, the book consists of radio reports and commentaries which I wrote as a Moscow correspondent from April 28, 1986 to April 26, 1989, the third anniversary of the catastrophe. The West German Broadcasting Company WDR was the main provider of my reports to almost 60 radio stations in West Germany. This company was responsible for the Moscow studio within the ARD[5], the network of public radio- and TV-stations in West Germany. I have also added to this book some of my articles for the Hamburg weekly newspaper *DIE ZEIT*[6]. This weekly did not have its own correspondent in Moscow at that time. During this period – two years after the accident – I made my only trip to the

---

[4] *Telegrafnoe Agenstvo Sovietskogo Sojusa* (News Agency of the Soviet Union).

[5] Working group of public broadcasters of the Federal Republic of Germany (Arbeitsgemeinschaft der öffentlich-rechtlichen Rundfunkanstalten in der Bundesrepublik Deutschland).

[6] These additional contributions are mentioned in footnotes.

exploded reactor unit of Chernobyl and the contaminated site of Pripyat, the former settlement of the Chernobyl workers.

These reports show in the beginning the helplessness of us journalists – Russian and foreign. The reason was simple. Many of the responsible personnel for the Chernobyl nuclear power plant falsified or even embezzled information intended for the central government and the Communist Party in Moscow. But after a while, *glasnost* then prevailed dramatically and a new type of investigative Soviet journalism emerged that traced the drama of Chernobyl in all its facets. This development can also be seen in contemporary reports.

In this book, the documentary part of contemporary reports is preceded by a brief chronological overview of the events as they can be written in retrospect and with the knowledge of many sources available today. This is followed by another brief chapter on the burdens that will continue to affect the contaminated areas and their inhabitants in the coming decades. With a shiver of horror, the reader will notice that today so-called "eye-opening" adventure tours into the "post-apocalyptic world" of Chernobyl and Pripyat are offered from Kiev. The book ends with the text of an almost 45-minute television conversation that the ARD-*alpha* educational channel recorded with me on the occasion of the 30th anniversary of the catastrophe. In this text one can understand both the uncertain assessment of the first days in April 1986 as well as the monstrous extent of this disaster and its consequences until today.

Overall, this book is a small contribution to the realistic handling of journalism in crises at a time when there was neither the internet, nor mobile phones, nor even e-mails or satellite television. My own research was limited for weeks to getting telephone contacts with people in the affected areas. There was no free telephone extension and the interlocutors on the other end of the phone were taped by "the services", as were we correspondents. So-called "informed circles" on the Soviet side also often proved to be chatterboxes who belittled the horror of the catastrophe.

The situation in Moscow was particularly tense for our families living with us. They sometimes experienced dramatic exaggerations via Western radio stations on short-wave transmitters or from Western newspapers[7] that arrived in Moscow days later. Occasionally they even wrote about

---

[7] Source of the newspaper illustration TODAY retrieved August 4, 2019 under http://mhill46-holdthefrontpage.blogspot.com/2011/08/nuclear-nightmare.html

thousands of alleged deaths that were "suspected" in the Soviet Union on the basis of measurement data in the West.

In this context, the letters of the German ambassador in Moscow to his compatriots living there are also interesting testimonies to contemporary history, which are also documented here thirty years later.

As correspondents from Moscow, we had to assert ourselves against hysteria in numerous Western tabloid media, which – contrary to better knowledge – spoke of an alleged death cloud over Europe and spread numbers of two thousand and more deaths as so-called established facts.

It was impossible for us as correspondents to prove the opposite. On the other hand, we could not confirm such assertions. [8]

---

[8] The headline of the German Tabloid BILD, retrieved July 21, 2020 under https://www.mediummagazin.de/1986-2011-die-katastrophen-in-tschernobyl-und-japan-im-spiegel-der-tagespresse/

The headlines[9] of that time demonstrate these irresponsible speculations as well as the challenge of reacting responsibly as journalists.

The reader must take into account that this is a journalistic book. The sources cited come from the current day's work, interviews, press conferences, background discussions, television and radio programs, as well as the daily and weekly newspapers from the years I worked as a foreign radio correspondent in the Soviet Union.

Newspapers, agencies and television programs cited on the reporting date are from the very same day.[10]

------

[9] Source of the newspaper illustration DAILY EXPRESS retrieved August 4, 2019 under https://www.forgottenchernobyl.net/chernobyl-coverage-in-daily-express-from-30-april-1986 (page 14).

[10] Articles and illustrations from the Soviet press about the Chernobyl catastrophe one can find under https://pripyat-city.ru/publications/169-pressa-ob-avarii-chast-ii.html, retrieved July 22, 2020.

DAILY EXPRESS

Wednesday April 30 1986 ● 20p (30p in Eire)

THE VOICE OF BRITAIN

Russia admits worst A-plant disaster ever

NUCLEAR NIGHTMARE IS HERE

- **More than 3,000 reported dead**
- **Thousands more are doomed**
- **Help us plea goes to the West**

By MICHAEL EVANS

AS MANY as 3,000 people could have died in the nightmare of the Russian nuclear disaster, Western diplomats in Moscow were reporting last night.

Ten thousand more could die from radiation and cancer.

One of the four reactors at the Chernobyl nuclear power complex 80 miles from Kiev is still burning.

Russia yesterday asked the West for help in dealing with the worst nuclear accident ever, despite the fact that Tass, the official Soviet newsagency, is claiming that only two people died.

Soviet sources quoted in New York put the figure at 2,100 dead. Another source in Kiev said up to 3,000 had died and 15,000 people were being evacuated from the area in hurriedly-commandeered buses and lorries.

RADIATION

Many may already be under sentence of death. Medical experts say there could be 10,000 fatalities over the next 20 years as radiation-induced cancers take their toll.

Britain appears to be safe. The sinister 40-mile high cloud of radiation which passed over Scandinavia is now being blown back across Russia—and over the North Pole towards America.

Water supplies are contaminated around Kiev.

Radiation-watchers at laboratories in Donreay, Harwell and Abingdon in Oxfordshire are still monitoring radioactivity levels

Suicide squads on edge of hell : Pages 2 and 3

THE LAST FAREWELL

THE Queen, the Queen Mother and other Royals made their farewells to the Duchess of Windsor. Jean Rook reports on Page 5.

SEALED WITH A KISS

KISSES from the stars of East-Enders as they celebrate winning the award of top BBC programme of the year. See Page 7.

CHRONOLOGY OF THE DISASTER

Until now, the Chernobyl disaster has been analyzed up to the minute, even to the second, by proponents[11] and opponents[12] and neutral observers[13] of nuclear energy.

We therefore know that on April 26, 1986, at one o'clock, twenty-three minutes and four seconds at night, a performance test was carried out in the fourth reactor unit. During this test the experts at the power station lost control. An emergency shutdown had failed. A fire broke out in the radioactive core of the reactor. At exactly 01:23:48 a.m. the

---

[11] This includes, above all, the International Atomic Energy Agency in Vienna, IAEA, which has maintained its own Chernobyl website for decades, retrieved August 4, 2019 under
https://www.iaea.org/newscenter/focus/chernobyl
With many other links, the IAEA also offers an insight into the state of research on Chernobyl, retrieved August 4, 2019 under
https://inis.iaea.org/search/search.aspx?orig_q=RN:19054937
[12] „The Chernobyl Catastrophe. Consequences on Human Health." 184 p. Published by Greenpeace 2006, retrieved August 4, 2019 under
https://www.sortirdunucleaire.org/IMG/pdf/greenpeace-2006-the_chernobyl_catastrophe-consequences_on_human_health.pdf
[13] Mostly journalistic publications like „Chernobyl Timeline: How a nuclear accident escalated to a historic disaster". By Jesse Greenspan. Retrieved August 4, 2019 under https://www.history.com/news/chernobyl-disaster-timeline.
The current state of discussion is reflected in the very extensive entry in Wikipedia, which also raises questions about the course of the first destruction of fuel rods or pressure tubes as well as the alternative explanations for the second explosion (oxyhydrogen gas or steam). Retrieved August 4, 2019 under
https:// https://en.wikipedia.org/wiki/Chernobyl_disaster

reactor exploded, i.e. not even one minute after the start of the test. This alone makes it clear how overwhelmed the responsible personnel in the reactor unit were. Not only had they made numerous wrong decisions, they also did not share information about the beginning catastrophe in time and completely.

The Soviet Union was not prepared in any way whatsoever for the onset of this catastrophe, which had been the biggest that had ever occurred in a nuclear power station worldwide. Following the registration in Sweden, Denmark and Finland of highly elevated radioactive measurements, the Soviet leadership had only a four-line message disseminated by the official news agency TASS confirming the accident succinctly.

The then Soviet party leader Mikhail Gorbachev, founder of the politics of *glasnost* and *perestroika*, let almost three weeks pass before he himself commented on the disaster on television. But the Soviet Union – and after the collapse of the USSR later Ukraine and Belarus – would still have decades to work on overcoming this catastrophe.

A remarkable document was found many years later in the Stasi documents of the GDR, i.e. the State Security of East Germany.[14] Officially, the government of the GDR – as well as Western states – had received no reliable information about the accident and its consequences. But on June 14, 1986, a good six weeks after the catastrophe, an unofficial collaborator for the Stasi, based in Moscow, under the code name "Werner Lorenz" gave a confidential, very detailed report. In the evening between 8 p.m. and 10 p.m. he met with Major Wohlleben of the GDR State Security, who made a stenographic transcript of the spoken conversation.

---

[14] The Stasi (Staatssicherheitsdienst) was the intelligence and secret police agency in the GDR, responsible for the gathering of information about internal affairs and political dissidents. It was the counterpart to the Soviet KGB.

This transcript, four pages in typewriter print, is about a meeting of the GDR Minister of Energy Wolfgang Mitzinger (*1932) with his Soviet colleague Anatoli Mayorets (1929-2016) and the chairman of the Soviet Committee for Atomic Energy, Andranik Petrosyants (1906-2005). With astonishing openness, for which Petrosyants later also became known in the West, this report already explains the exact sequence of the catastrophe, the misconduct of those responsible and the deficits in the manufacture of nuclear reactors in the USSR.

There is already information in this report, which only became known to the public months later. During this conversation, the Soviet side attached importance to the fact that Chernobyl was purely an accident due to a lack of technical mastery of the operational procedures, but not an act of sabotage. Because of the explosive nature of the information shared at this meeting, a copy of two facsimiles are documented here.[15] The document is titled as: "Conversation between the Secretaries of energy of the GDR and the Soviet Union about the nuclear disaster of Chernobyl". The first facsimile shows the date and time of the meeting between the secret informant and the major of the Stasi. Further on, it confirms that the informant in Moscow provided information about the Chernobyl accident for the GDR government. The second facsimile is the beginning of the protocol which is documented in translation.

---

[15] The original document can be found in the Stasi Media Archives of the Federal Commissioner for the records of the State Security Service of the former German Democratic Republic. This protocol is written in a very bureaucratic language. Signature: BstU, MfS, AIM, No. 16005/89, Part II, pages 260-265. Metadata: Service unit: Department XVIII, date 19.6.1986. Retrieved August 4, 2019 under
https://www.stasi-mediathek.de/medien/gespraech-der-energieminister-der-ddr-und-sowjetunion-ueber-das-reaktorunglueck-von-tschernobyl/blatt/260/

Gespräch der Energieminister der DDR und Sowjetunion über das Reaktorunglück von Tschernobyl

Diensteinheit HA XVIII/3/2

−242−

BSTU 0260

Datum 19.06.86

Treffbericht

Sichtvermerke
Obj. 19.06.86
d. 23.6.86
Hg 25.6.86

Kategorie/Deckname IMS „Werner Lorenz"

Datum/Zeit	Treffort	Mitarbeiter	Teilnahme durch Vorgesetzten
14.06.86 20⁰⁰−22⁰⁰ h	Wohnung des IM	Major Nittleben	

Nächster Treff	am	Zeit	Treffort
erfolgt durch OG Moskau			

Ausweichtreff	am	Zeit	Treffort

Treffvorbereitung:
(z. B. Treff geplant / kurzfristig festgelegt, Kurzfassung des geplanten Treffablaufes, Schwerpunkte der Auftragserteilung, Instruierung, Erziehung und Befähigung)

Der Treff wurde kurzfristig im Zusammenhang mit einem Zwischenaufenthalt des IM in der DDR vereinbart. (IM befindet sich z.Zt. im Auslandseinsatz)
Es war vorgesehen, daß der IM prät. zu Hinweise zur Havarie und ihren Schlußfolgerungen im KKW Tschernobyl erarbeitet.

Signatur: BStU, MfS, AIM, Nr. 16005/89, Teil II, Bl. 260-265

Blatt 260

espräch der Energieminister der DDR und Sowjetunion über das Reaktorunglück von Tschernobyl

-243-

BSTU
0262

Anlage zum Treffbericht IMS "Werner Lorenz"
vom 14. Juni 1986 - Politisch-operative Hinweise
zur Havarie im KKW Tschernobyl

In einem am 3. Juni 1986 zwischen dem Minister für Kohle
und Energie, Gen. Mitzinger, und dem Minister für
Energetik und Elektrifizierung der UdSSR, Gen. Majorez,
sowie dem Vorsitzenden des Staatlichen Komitees für die
Nutzung der Atomenergie der UdSSR, Gen. Prof. Petrosjanz,
in Moskau geführten internen Gespräch informierte die
sowjetische Seite über die Ursachen, Umstände und Be-
dingungen der am 26. April 1986 eingetretenen Havarie im
KKW Tschernobyl:

-   In der Nacht vom 25. zum 26. April 1986 erfolgte zur
Durchführung prophylaktischer Zustandsüberprüfungen des
Blockes 4 (1ooo MW elektrische Leistung; 3ooo MW thermische
Leistung) die planmäßige Außerbetriebnahme.
Während des Abfahrprozesses dieses Blockes wurde gleichzeitig
in Abweichung von dem normalen Betriebszustand das Verhalten
der Anlage bei Ausfall der Elektroenergieversorgung aus dem
öffentlichen Netz für die Eigenbedarfsversorgung getestet
(Feststellung, inwieweit die Auslaufenergie der Turbine /
Generator für den Betrieb der Hauptumwälzpumpen zur Kühlung /
Wärmeabführung aus dem Reaktor über eine kurze Zeit bis zur
Einschaltung der Notstromversorgung ausreicht).
Der Reaktor hatte zu diesem Zeitpunkt eine thermische Leistung
von über 2oo MWth (das entspricht ca. 7 % der thermischen
Nennleistung) und von den vorhandenen 6 Umwälzpumpen waren
nur 3 in Betrieb. Bei der Durchführung dieses Versuchsprogramms
kam es zu örtlichen Überhitzungen in der Brennstoffzone des
Reaktors (Kühlung reichte offensichtlich nicht aus), was durch
den Reaktoroperator bemerkt wurde.

Annex to the Meeting Report with the informant
"Werner Lorenz" of June 14, 1986.
Political-operational notes on the accident
at the
Chernobyl Nuclear Power Plant

In a meeting held on June 3, 1986 between the Minister of Coal and Energy, General Mitzinger, and the Minister of Energy and Electrification of the USSR, Gen. Mayorets, and the Chairman of the State Committee for the Use of Atomic Energy of the USSR, Gen. Prof. Petrosyants, an internal meeting held in Moscow, the Soviet side informed about the causes, circumstances and conditions of the accident at the Chernobyl nuclear power plant that occurred on April 26, 1986.

– In the night from April 25-26, 1986, the scheduled shutdown operation was carried out in order to implement prophylactic status condition checks of unit 4 (1,000 MW electrical power; 3,000 MB thermal power).

During the shutdown of this unit the behavior of the plant in the event of a failure of the electrical power supply from the public grid for emergency power supply was tested deviating from the normal operation (determination of the extent to which the turbine / generator run-out energy for the operation of the main circulation pumps for cooling / heat dissipation from the reactor is sufficient for a short time until the emergency power supply is switched on).

At this time the reactor had a thermal power of more than 200 MWth (this corresponds to approx. 7% of the nominal thermal power) and only 3 of the 6 circulating pumps were in operation. During the execution of this test program, local overheating occurred in the fuel zone of the reactor (cooling was obviously not sufficient), which was noticed by the reactor operator.

(Page 2)

The reactor operator then switched on the main circulating pumps which were not in operation with the aim of increasing the water flow for cooling/heat dissipation in the reactor.

This resulted in an uncontrollable increase in the output of the reactor, which was not controlled by the control system. The control ability of the reactor was restricted by clamping control rods.

On the part of the Soviet experts, it cannot be ruled out that the control rods may get stuck in the protective and safety drive system of the reactor due to the lack of guide rails.

Under these operating conditions (overheating of the fuel zone, uncontrolled power increase, reactivation of main circulating pumps), an explosive hydrogen-oxygen mixture (so-called oxyhydrogen gas) was formed and thus a high overpressure was generated, causing the reactor to explode and result in a fire.

A large part of the radioactive material was thrown up out of the reactor and released.

The Chernobyl NPP[16] does not have a safety containment (containment or pressure vessel) to

---

16 NPP Nuclear Power Plant.

withstand radioactive nuclides from the environment for such accidents.

Around 100,000 people had to be evacuated in the vicinity of the NPP.

So far, about 30 deaths have occurred.

The main cause of the serious accident in the Chernobyl NPP was given by the Soviet side as the lack of control of the reactor operation under the given conditions. The investigations showed that acts of sabotage can be excluded.

The damaged reactor was or is provided with a hermetic seal.

To prevent overheating as a result of the radioactive decay processes that are still taking place, cooling and ventilation systems are being set up in the emergency area.

(Page 3)

The risk of groundwater contamination was eliminated by reinforcing the foundations.

It is planned to restart the 1,000 MW units 1 and 2 in the Chernobyl NPP in October 1986.

When fighting the accident, robot technology from the NSW (e.g. dump trucks, tractors) with remote control were used.

According to statements from the Soviet side, this technology has not proved itself in terms of reliability.

According to the results of the investigations to date, there were a number of deficiencies and favorable conditions with regard to the occurrence and control of the accident.

To this end, conclusions capable of generalization are being drawn up by the responsible Soviet organs and institutions.

In this context, the following fundamental problems were pointed out by the Soviet side:

– The carrying out of experiments or tests in nuclear power plants must be thoroughly prepared on a scientific and technical basis and coordinated with the higher-level state and supervising bodies.

(In the case of the Chernobyl nuclear power plant, the test program was only prepared and implemented in-house.)

– The order, safety, discipline and qualification of personnel must be raised to a significantly higher level and enforced according to military principles.

– Greater attention should be paid to the psychological preparation of the operating personnel for the control of disturbances and accidents in order to prevent panic-like reactions and behavior in the future.

– The forces and means for special fire fighting must meet the special requirements in the nuclear power plant, i.e. also in the case of melting of the nuclear fuel zone.

(At the Chernobyl nuclear power plant, the operational fire brigade was not sufficiently qualified for this purpose).

The information systems must be fully functional in the event of hazards, malfunctions, accidents and fires and meet the requirements in terms of what needs to be done and when.

(In the event of the accident at the Chernobyl nuclear power plant, for example, the Minister of Energy and Electrification of the USSR was informed belatedly that Reactor 4 was no longer fully operational.

In order to improve the bilateral exchange of information between the USSR and the GDR on experiences and findings in the operation of nuclear power plants, it is planned to conclude an agreement between the ministries involved.

To this end, special collectives are to be formed with the involvement of experts.

– The Soviet side is striving to form an international intervention force of the socialist countries to combat nuclear power plant accidents and eliminate the consequences of accidents.

– Scientific and technical research in the field of nuclear safety at nuclear power stations should be stepped up.

(Note: Internally, the Chairman of the State Committee for the Use of Atomic Energy of the USSR, Gen. Prof. Petrosyants, expressed that e.g. scientific-technical investigations are necessary for the safety of interim storage facilities for spent nuclear fuel, taking into account possible changes in the condition of the materials used. At the present time, no reliable statement can be made as to whether it is still possible to transport the nuclear fuel assemblies after a long period of storage.)

The Soviet side expressed the view that after the accident at the Chernobyl nuclear power plant, no cuts will be made in the use of nuclear energy for power generation (electricity and heat) in the USSR.

Further investigations are being carried out in the USSR on the use of the graphite-moderated pressure-tube generator – as in the Chernobyl nuclear power plant – and the associated safety systems.

(Note: According to GDR experts, this reactor type represents a technical interim solution, taking into account the lower economic and technical costs compared to other reactor types of this power size. One of the reasons for this technical interim solution is that the production capacities for the manufacture of reactor pressure vessels in the USSR are in a bottleneck.)

(signature)

Wohlleben, Major

After Chernobyl, in the then Soviet Union had occurred what has never happened in the past:

The public began a critical debate on nuclear energy. However, the accelerated expansion of nuclear power was continued by Soviet economic planning.

In addition, experts had to eliminate existing and identifiable risks that had been demonstrated in the previous practice of Soviet nuclear power plants. This was particularly true of the Chernobyl reactor type, which had not been rebuilt since the accident. The concrete consequence of this was the decision that the two additionally planned reactor units at Chernobyl would no longer be completed. Finally, the nuclear power plant of Chernobyl has been shut down totally.

In Smolensk and Kursk, according to initial reports, two other nuclear power units were shut down, using the same technology as the Chernobyl nuclear power plant. All 14 units of the same type dating from the 1970s had to be modernized and equipped with additional safety features. Further reactor units at the Beloyarsk and Novovoronezh nuclear power plants were allegedly being prepared for decommissioning. The only nuclear power plant operated in Armenia in the immediate vicinity of the capital Yerevan was completely shut down after the severe earthquake in 1988.

A previously unthinkable information policy for the Soviet Union had been implemented: Nuclear power plants were opened for regular visits; company representatives, training facilities, public organizations – all of them were now to receive on-the-spot instruction on nuclear energy. An information center for nuclear energy was established in Moscow, and public discussions on nuclear energy were held regularly in a specialized institute.

Nevertheless, these measures were not sufficient to minimize the horrors of Chernobyl and, at the same time, to persuade the population toward the future development concerning the use of nuclear energy.

On the third anniversary of the catastrophe the party newspaper *Pravda* devoted a whole page to the problems of radioactive contamination, which is still effective. For illustration purposes, the newspaper printed three maps from the Chernobyl catchment area, in which detailed measurements of the contamination were recorded. In a conclusion, the Soviet minister for environmental issues Yuri Izrael (1930-2014) stated that "the radioactive contamination of the environment on a considerable territory will still remain a serious technical and social problem".[17]

For the first time in three years, Mikhail Gorbachev also ventured to Chernobyl, where Gorbachev – in white protective clothing – had the shift supervisor explain the work sequence to him in the first reactor unit of the nuclear power plant. The party leader always interrupted when safety issues were at stake. "Did the new automatic system really work? Is it now possible to rule out errors?"

Gorbachev then spoke to the workers at the nuclear power plant. Their concerns: shortcomings in medical care. "And the Soviet press", they complained, "polemicizes insensitively against nuclear energy". In the role of an advocate of the public, Gorbachev replied: "In a way, you need to understand the press. The public concerns and mistrust are justified."[18]

In the newly built town of Slavutych, where Chernobyl employees were accommodated after the catastrophe, the party leader held a lesson in nuclear energy in front of the camera using the methods of a senior teacher. He called on experts to explain in a few sentences what's bothering them and what they expect from nuclear energy.

---

[17] *Pravda*, April 26, 1986.
[18] Soviet TV, First Channel, February 21, 1989.

The Chernobyl plant director asked for more qualified attention from the mass media and praised nuclear power as "the cleanest thing we have ecologically"[19]. The chief scientist of the Soviet Academy of Sciences, Yevgeny Velikhov, saw no chance to cover the Soviet energy requirements without nuclear power and demanded that society should adapt to it.

The Ukrainian politician Boris Shcherbina (1919-1990), head of the Catastrophe Commission at the time, simply said: "Young people must learn to observe regulations better so that an accident like Chernobyl does not repeat itself." And the environmental chief of the government Yuri Izrael confirmed that one could already live again in parts of the restricted zones, where only certain types of mushrooms were not allowed to be eaten.[20]

Shortly after Gorbachev's visit to Chernobyl, the weekly *Moskovskiye Novosti* had reported on the actual catastrophic long-term consequences, which began to appear at the same time. A reporter had visited a collective farm in the catchment area of the radioactive contamination. A frightening increase in malformations was noted on the livestock farms there. The report concerning about 440 head of cattle reads literally:

"In the five years before Chernobyl altogether three cases of physical abnormalities among the piglets were registered. There were none among the calves at all.

But already within the first year after the accident 64 malformed animals were born. 37 piglets and 27 calves were born without heads and extremities, eyes or ribs".[21]

Among the human population the number of miscarriages more than doubled. According to the newspaper, 76 cases were registered in the two years following the catastrophe.

---

[19] ibid.

[20] ibid.

[21] *Moskovskiye Novosti*, No 9, 1989.

And these figures come only from a single collective farm in a more distant region of the disaster area.

Such publications are unsettling above all for women, who are pregnant or want to become pregnant. The responsible Ministry of Health in Kiev has long maintained the statement that there is no longer any danger outside the immediate Chernobyl radiation zone.

"If there is no longer any danger, as we are repeatedly told", the weekly newspaper *Moskovskiye Novosti* quoted one affected woman, "why are we advised against pregnancy?" Finally, the paper referred to a representative of the local administration in the Zhitomir area, which lies far outside the so-called danger zone. According to him, the medical staff has noticed a significant increase in chronic illnesses. It is said that recovery times are getting longer and longer after surgical interventions. And further, literally: "Also, the annual average of cancer cases has doubled – above all, we have noticed this in lip and mouth cancer."[22]

On the fourth anniversary of the catastrophe in 1990, Soviet television reported for 24 hours on the terrible consequences for people in the Chernobyl catchment area. Desperate mothers held their injured and handicapped children up to the camera and accused the state, which had left the people alone in their misery.[23]

---

[22] ibid.

[23] Due to the nature of live reporting, some facts mentioned here are repeated chronologically as part of the reports under the single dates later in this book.

BURDENS FOR THE FUTURE

Ukraine, a model of economic and technological performance in the former Soviet Union, experienced its bitterest lesson of the post-war period in April 1986 with the catastrophe at the Chernobyl nuclear power plant, which continues to have an effect today.[24] The consequences of the disaster continue to weigh on the state of Ukraine, which has been independent since 1991, but also on the state of Belarus, which has also been independent since 1991. For years to come, fears and rumors have affected the social climate in Ukraine. Chernobyl became a severe test for the then just begun phase of Mikhail Gorbachev's reform policy with *glasnost*, the new openness:

On the one hand the Soviet authorities lacked for a long time exact knowledge about the course of the accident and its

---

[24] For the ecological consequences check the trilingual (Russian, Ukrainian, English) homepage *International Chernobyl Research and Information Network*. Retrieved August 4, 2019 under

http://www.chernobyl.info/Default.aspx?tabid=120

It also contains projections for the effects of the radioactive fallout of cesium, strontium and transuranium until 2055, i.e. 70 years after the catastrophe.

The IAEA offers a summary of the work of this research group under the title: "Environmental Consequences of the Chernobyl Accident and their Remediation: Twenty Years of Experience". 180 p. Retrieved August 4, 2019 under

https://www-pub.iaea.org/MTCD/publications/PDF/Pub1239_web.pdf

consequences, on the other hand it turned out only after four years that much available information had actually been withheld. Even before that – at a medical conference in Kiev in 1988 – Swedish and American scientists in particular had criticized the fact that there was still no data available on actual radiation exposure and that there was no precise list of the group of people at risk for late complications.

A year later, Yuri Izrael, then Chairman of the State Committee for Hydrology and Meteorology, announced that approximately 230,000 people lived in the Chernobyl contaminated area. In 1990, the Vice-President of the Environmental Commission of the Soviet Parliament finally admitted that in the area with excessive radioactive contamination there were in fact as many as four million people, 1.5 million of whom had been exposed to a "high dose of radiation", including 160,000 children. Late effects were noticeable: thyroid cancer, leukemia, blood diseases, rising numbers of stillbirths and high infant mortality. Four years after the catastrophe, experts called for the evacuation of at least 118 settlement points, mainly in the bordering region of Belarus, because the radiation exposure there was unbearably high.

One must keep it in mind, that the border of Belarus is only twelve miles from Chernobyl. And that a greater part of the nuclear fallout was blown by the wind to Belarus.

The follow-up costs of Chernobyl have only been accurately estimated over the years. They meant an additional burden for the tense situation of the then Soviet Union and its affected successor states. By the turn of the millennium, the equivalent of 300 billion US dollars had been estimated if the damage caused by the catastrophe was to be completely repaired. Chernobyl, which should have become the largest nuclear power plant in the world, became one of the most expensive ruins of the nuclear industry.

Even years after the catastrophe, on a journey from Kiev to Chernobyl – about 80 miles north – one had to be prepared for a shocking experience. A few miles from Chernobyl, the richly wooded landscape turned into a desert. Trees and bushes had simply died. The earth around the complex of the nuclear power plant had been removed to a depth of more than eight inches and the ground had been refilled with fresh sand.

It was not until years later that time was found for a critical stock-taking. The head of the Information Department at the Chernobyl nuclear power plant Aleksandr Kovalenko took the questions of the few authorized correspondents who were allowed to visit the power plant in 1988. Right away he started with the shortcomings: During the salvage work immediately after the catastrophe, there had been disputes over competence because forty (!) different ministries were involved and had each asserted their say. Finally, a separate office was set up to repair the damage, professionally organized and without any disputes over competence.

"You have five minutes to visit the sarcophagus," reminded the power plant spokesman at the time, pressing a radiometer into my hand. This allowed me to venture up to about 200 yards to the burst ruins of the fourth reactor unit, which – enclosed by a skin of lead – actually resembled a sarcophagus. The measuring device reacted differently depending on the direction of the wind.

After the catastrophe, the Chernobyl workers lived in their own settlement, named Selyony Mys, about 30 miles away. 10,000 workers and 3,000 builders were reinstated in the nuclear power plant as long as it was unclear what would happen to Chernobyl and before the decision was made to shut it down completely. Soldiers took over the decontamination, removing the earth and flushing the radioactive fallout from roofs and streets in the nearby town of Pripyat, from where the entire population had been evacuated. In the danger zone, work was carried out by so-called liquidators at 15-day intervals, after which the workers were released for another 15 days. The normal risk bonus for dangerous operations was doubled. When the maximum permitted dose of radiation was reached, the liquidators had to hand over their work to a fresh crew. In this manner, approximately 600,000 workers were involved in the clearing of the disaster site.[25]

With increasing openness *(glasnost)*, Chernobyl became the subject of highly critical scrutiny by the Soviet press. There was talk of binge drinking among the workers, of a new sloppiness and even the hiring of former criminals. But only one month after the catastrophe, in May 1986, 14,000 applications had been received, allegedly from volunteers who wanted to help in Chernobyl. "We did not choose according to party affiliation," said the power plant's press chief, alluding to later accusations, "but according to the characteristic of sympathy and pity. But then masses of officials came and began to look at who had been convicted, who had been expelled from the Communist Party and so on."[26]

Especially for the party newspaper *Pravda*, press chief Kovalenko had nothing good to say about the paper because *Pravda* had repeatedly attacked the conditions for the liquidators in Chernobyl. He tried historical comparisons with overthrown party figures to discredit *Pravda's* critical attitude:

"In the 1920s Trotsky made a mistake in this newspaper, in the 1930s Bukharin, in the 1960s Stalin's cult was exposed, in the 1970s Brezhnev's glory was praised and empty straw was threshed and at the beginning of the 1980s they set about exposing that too. Oh well, I forgot about Zhdanov, who was wrong in the forties."[27]

---

[25] Retrieved May 11, 2020 under
https://en.wikipedia.org/wiki/Chernobyl_liquidators
[26] Interview with the author May 12, 1988.
[27] ibid.

But it would have been more important if the criticism of the hasty construction and sloppiness at the Chernobyl Nuclear power plant, which had even appeared in a Ukrainian trade journal and in the local press before the catastrophe, had been taken into account.

The name CHORNOBYL TOUR is registered as a trademark.

But the impending energy shortage confronting the Soviet Union had played a major role in making nuclear energy the focus of a hasty expansion program, regardless of its possible consequences.

What remained in Chernobyl – apart from the long-term ecological and health consequences – was a new high-tech sarcophagus built in 2016 for around 1.6 billion dollars. For the next 100 years, it will hide around 180 tons of contaminated and still radioactive material.

What is left behind, however, is a rather depressing sensationalism about earning money with the horrors of Chernobyl.

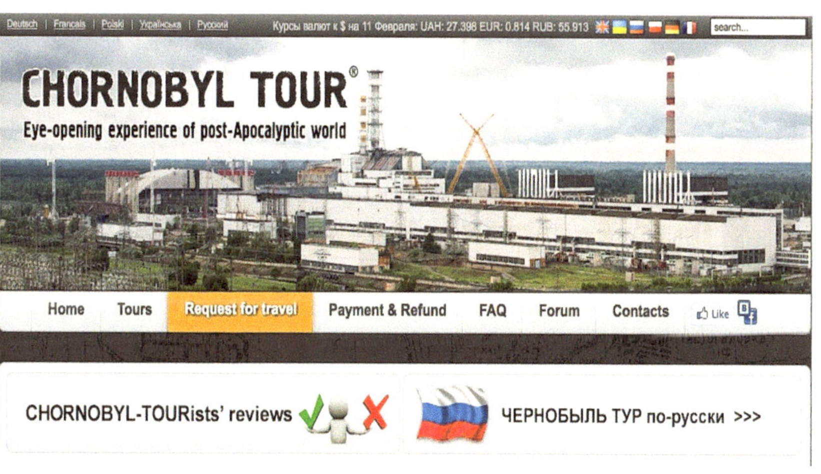

Early on, the media complained that souvenir hunters plundered the ruins of the nuclear power plant and the town of Pripyat in order to sell metal parts from "buried" clearing equipment, helicopters, cranes, cars or simply furniture from the contaminated apartments on the black market.

In the meantime, an "orderly" branch of tourism has emerged in Ukraine. A so-called "Chernobyl Tour – Eye-opening experience of post-Apocalyptic world" is advertised on the streets of Kiev with posters and blackboards as well as on the internet – even with reference to TripAdvisor.

The corresponding website[28] offers not only a tour inside the Chernobyl nuclear power plant, but also a "military tour: shooting range, armored reconnaissance patrol vehicle".

This tour is literally advertised on the Ukrainian homepage with the following text:

"Shooting range is a place where you get an opportunity to correctly and wisely use the firearms. CHORNOBYL TOUR® along with the shooting range management and well-qualified shooting instructors suggest you get shooting experience from legendary AK-57, AKM, Kalashnikov LMG, world-known American M-16 rifles and M-4 carbines, Dragunov sniper rifles and the newest Ukrainian half-automatic Z-10 rifles, a prototype of American AR-10. Apart from this, F-500 pump-action shotguns, Makarov pistols, Fort revolver, CZ-75, Fort-21, Glock-17, and small-caliber Margolin and Taurus pistols are also available."[29]

In the meantime even airplane tours are possible, advertised with an impressive view of the nuclear power plant from the air.[30]

Souvenirs of all kinds – like these magnetic pictures – are available to remind tourists of the horrors of the catastrophe.[31]

---

[28] Retrieved August 4, 2019 under http://chernobyl-tour.ua/
The spelling of the link address *Chernobyl* follows the English transcription of the Russian name Чернобыль, which is also found in most English book titles. In the text, however, the homepage partly follows the Ukrainian spelling Чорнобиль, in Latin letters paraphrased as *Chornobyl*.
[29] Retrieved August 4, 2019 under http://chernobyl-tour.ua/ shooting_range_tour_kiev_en.html
[30] Retrieved August 7,2020 under https://www.chernobyl-tour.com/chornobyl_air_tour_en.html (Illustration page 37)
[31] Retrieved August 7, 2020 under https://www.chernobyl-tour.com/souvenirs_en.html (Illustration page 37)

Airplane tours over Chernobyl

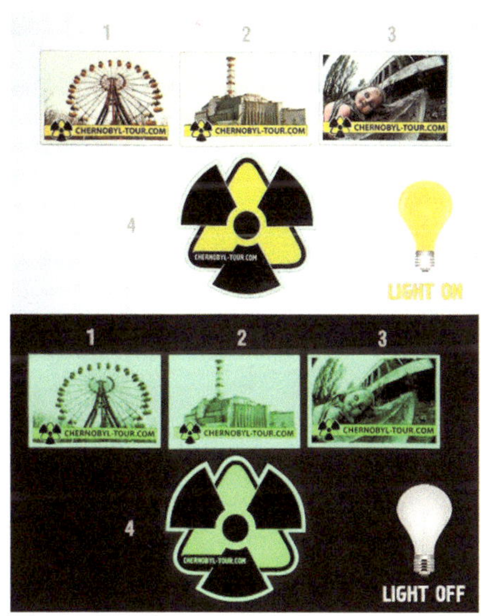

Magnet pictures as souvenirs

Invitation in Kiev to the Chernobyl tour.

HOW IT ALL BEGAN

In Western Europe rising radioactive values were measured, which – according to the air flow – have to had originated clearly from the Soviet Union. But the official sources in Moscow were silent, until TASS published the following message nearly two days after the accident:

TASS Message APRIL 28, 1986
9:02 p.m. Moscow time

Only these four lines were read at the same time on the

```
282102 APR 86


          NNNN
ZCZC XOS733


   .NUCLEAR POWER PLANT--USSR COUNCIL OF MINISTERS.
   28/4 TASS 4-53


   MOSCOW APRIL 28 TASS - AN ACCIDENT HAS OCCURRED AT THE
CHERNOBYL ATOMIC POWER PLANT AS ONE OF THE ATOMIC REACTORS WAS
DAMAGED.
   MEASURES ARE BEING UNDERTAKEN TO ELIMINATE THE CONSEQUENCES
OF THE ACCIDENT. AID IS BEING GIVEN TO THOSE AFFECTED.
   A GOVERNMENT COMMISSION HAS BEEN SET UP.
   ITEM ENDS """
```

evening TV news broadcast *Vremja*, starting 9 p.m. Moscow time. Hardly an hour later, TASS did not add further information on the Chernobyl accident, but published in two parts a five times longer report on incidents at nuclear power plants in the USA. TASS classified Chernobyl as the first reactor accident ever in the Soviet Union, which then was contrasted with 2,300 incidents in the USA alone in one year. This relativization was intended to reassure the public.

<table>
<tr><td>

TASS Message APRIL 28, 1986[32]
9:58 p.m. Moscow time

</td></tr>
</table>

```
                    NNNN
ZCZC MOS746 NNNN
ZCZC MOS747 NNNN
ZCZC MOS748

   .ATOMIC POWER STATIONS--ACCIDENTS #1.
   (TWO TAKES)
   28/4 TASS 4-54

   MOSCOW APRIL 28 TASS - THE ACCIDENT AT THE CHERNOBYL ATOMIC
POWER STATION IS THE FIRST ONE IN THE SOVIET UNION. SIMILAR
ACCIDENTS HAPPENED ON SEVERAL OCCASIONS IN OTHER COUNTRIES.
   IN THE UNITED STATES, 2,300 ACCIDENTS, BREAKDOWNS AND OTHER
FAULTS WERE REGISTERED IN 1979 ALONE, ACCORDING TO THE PUBLIC
ORGANIZATION CALLED CRITICAL MASS.
   THE MAJOR CAUSES OF THE DANGEROUS SITUATION ARE THE POOR
QUALITY OF REACTORS AND OTHER TYPES OF EQUIPMENT, UNSATISFACTO
CONTROL OVER THE TECHNICAL CONDITION OF THE EQUIPMENT,
NON-OBSERVANCE OF SAFETY REGULATIONS AND INSUFFICIENT
PROFESSIONAL TRAINING OF PERSONNEL.
   THE ATOMIC POWER STATION NORTH ANNA-1, VIRGINIA, NEAR
WASHINGTON D.C., IS TOPPING THE LIST OF ACCIDENT-PRONE STATION

   MORE
```

---

[32] The Critical Mass Energy Project was the umbrella organization of an anti-nuclear movement in the USA, founded in 1974 by Ralph Nader. Retrieved August 4, 2019 under
https://en.wikipedia.org/wiki/Critical_Mass_Energy_Project)

```
                    NNNN
ZCZC NOS754 NNNN
ZCZC NOS755

 *   .ATOMIC POWER STATIONS--ACCIDENTS #2.

    28/4 TASS 4-54

    A MAJOR ACCIDENT OCCURRED IN 1979 AT THE ATOMIC POWER
STATION IN HARRISBURG, PENNSYLVANIA, WHERE RADIOACTIVE
SUBSTANCES LEAKED DUE TO A REACTOR BREAKDOWN.
    AS A RESULT, RADIOACTIVITY RAISED TO A LEVEL DANGEROUS TO
HUMAN HEALTH. IN ORDER TO AVOID CASUALTIES, THE LOCAL
AUTHORITIES WERE COMPELLED TO EVACUATE THOUSANDS OF RESIDENTS
FROM THE AREA AROUND THE STATION AND NEARBY REGIONS.
    A YEAR LATER, EIGHT PEOPLE WERE DOUSED WITH RADIOACTIVE
WATER AS A HOSE BECAME TORN DURING MAINTENANCE WORK AT THE
ATOMIC POWER PLANT IN ZION, ILLINOIS. OVERALL, 40,000 LITRES OF
CONTAMINATED WATER POURED INTO THE ATOMIC PLANT BUILDING.
    SIMILAR ACCIDENTS ALSO WERE REGISTERED AT THE ATOMIC POWER
STATION NEAR NEW YORK CITY, AT THE ATOMIC POWER PLANT IN AIKEN,
SOUTH CAROLINA, AND SOME OTHERS.
    ITEM ENDS """
```

In retrospect, it is both astonishing and frightening that the
deficiencies mentioned in these reports, which were attributed
to the American nuclear power plants, also applied to an even
greater extent to the Chernobyl disaster. Without knowing it,
TASS had thus practically anticipated the analysis of the
Chernobyl accident.

THE YEAR 1986

April 29, 1986

IN THE PRESS – NOT A WORD

The reports from the disaster area are sparse. Some correspondents have been able to telephone with the Ukrainian capital Kiev, which is about 80 miles south of Chernobyl.

According to this information, there is no exceptional situation in Kiev. The city seems to be quiet. It is said that there is no evidence of evacuation measures. Foreign embassies in Moscow have also received similar information.

On the outskirts of Kiev, the staff of a German company is working, which has contacted the Moscow Foreign Ministry via the German embassy in order to obtain possible rules of conduct in the event of a disaster. A reaction from the Foreign Ministry in Moscow is not yet available.

The Soviet press does not report the accident today with a single line.

The short, only four-line message of the Soviet agency TASS has not yet been reprinted anywhere. Also, the Soviet radio news – as far as one can tell – has not yet dealt with the disaster.

Only one year ago the Soviet Union signed an agreement with the International Atomic Energy Agency in Vienna. Since then, Soviet nuclear power plants may be inspected by commissions from other countries. For the first time, following this agreement, an international commission of experts travelled to Moscow to inspect two nuclear power plants near the Soviet capital. The Soviet Union had already entered into an obligation to report disturbances at facilities – whether civil or military – when it joined the International Atomic Energy Agency.

The Soviet media's reluctance to respond to disasters in their own country is typical. In most cases, only events such as earthquakes or major environmental pollution are reported that are already identifiable by international measurements. On the other hand, there are usually no reports about air or train accidents within the Soviet Union.

In the case of real natural disasters, however, reports in recent years have increasingly come from the crisis region within the Soviet Union. However, accidents in Western countries – anything from a hotel fire to a train collision – are usually reported in the Soviet news.

THE SILENCE CONTINUES

The news of deaths and injuries, of radioactive contamination and evacuation of the population is not top news in the Soviet Union.

The evening television program praised the new fashion line with lyrical breadth. A new diesel-powered truck model also took precedence, not to mention a new electricity link between the socialist brother countries and the usual reports of successful field work.

Only then did the speaker's face darken to announce the new version from the Council of Ministers about the accident. The world has not become wiser as a result.

When and to what extent what happened remains a secret: the cause of the accident, the amount of radioactivity leaked, the number of injured and evacuees. Accuracy in this case is not a matter of Soviet information.

But the concession that there have been two deaths already has a shock effect on Soviet citizens, regardless of whether there may have been several more deaths. The very term "dead" in a disaster in one's own country is unusual and therefore frightening enough.

Two young Muscovites, in their early twenties, commented on the fact that the radioactive cloud had also spread over other countries and that the Soviet Union admitted the disaster only with delay and under international pressure:

"Typically, what happens in our country is always the last thing we learn ourselves."

So far, Soviet citizens have not learned anything about the contacts of Soviet diplomats and scientists with experts from abroad. Whether requests for help have really been made and foreign specialists will have access to the scene of the accident cannot be confirmed from Moscow.

How differently did the Soviet media behave during the accident at the American nuclear power plant at Three Mile Island near Harrisburg, PA.[33] From the very beginning, there were reports and comments in detail. The conclusion: Catastrophes in capitalist foreign countries are always good to show what a dying branch the class enemy is sitting on.

---

[33] Three Mile Island is known for having been the site of the most significant accident in US commercial nuclear energy, on March 28, 1979, when 2 suffered a partial meltdown.

DECEPTION

Almost three years ago a South Korean jumbo jet had been shot down by Soviet fighter planes. Moscow insisted for a week on this version:

An unknown aircraft had penetrated Soviet airspace and then disappeared towards the Sea of Japan.

When the shooting was finally admitted, a Kremlin spokesman rebuked protesting Western journalists in a press conference:

"Please don't accuse official authorities in Moscow of having lied before. If you do so," the argument goes, "you don't understand our political language properly."

Indeed, the Kremlin's news policy did not lie at the time. But they did not tell the truth either. And this is precisely where the dilemma of Soviet information policy lies.

If an airplane disappears, then we cannot rule out the possibility that it has been shot down. Or, in relation to the current case: If – as we are told in fine linguistic detail - two people died during the accident at the Chernobyl nuclear power plant, then further radiation victims are not unthinkable.

Dealing with Soviet information teaches us to play with a logic that is different by Western standards.

In the event of disasters in the Soviet Union, one must always look for things that have not been mentioned or denied.

The public statements by party and government, supposed to have such a calming and non-binding effect on the outside, trigger only rumors, dismay and additional false information.

Whoever relies on the Russian babushka from the countryside, who crosses herself three times and has seen dozens of dead in a traffic accident, where in reality only a donkey cart collided with a bike – in view of such information deficits – is just as badly advised as by some news presentation from *Pravda*.

In a disaster like Chernobyl, however, all ironic remarks must be banned. It is not only a sign of recklessness, but also of an unusual cynicism that the world's public is put off with the thin claim that there have been some outflows of radioactive substances; and further on, the either meaningless or revealing claim that the radioactive situation has stabilized.

If, with a measurably increased radioactivity in the air in several countries hundreds of miles away from the scene of the accident, the perpetrator does not have the courage to tell the truth, he loses his credibility.

Gorbachev's slogan *glasnost* – openness – still is ringing in people's ears: All things in public life – the party leader has promised and demanded – must be treated with relentless openness. His offers on disarmament measures and their international controls will now be determined on this one point: If the Soviet Union does not have the courage to accept this self-proclaimed openness in the event of a civil disaster, how will it proceed in the military arena?

The standard that is now being applied cannot be strict enough. Chernobyl is not somewhere in Eastern Siberia, far away from other national borders. Chernobyl is no longer an internal affair of the Soviet Union. Nobody in Moscow should really want to talk his way out of the often-attempted slogan of non-interference. Chernobyl lies – to put it in a nutshell – in the middle of Europe and is no further from Vienna than the French capital Paris.

The Soviet Union has always had to accept criticism of its information policy. In contrast, it has often relied on its well-coordinated propaganda machine and did not rule out further misleading information.

With media-effective appearances by an agile party leader, with open press conferences and self-criticism, a start was made that gave many hope for improvement.

These hopes are destroyed with such wrong decisions, which already now prevent the clearing-up of Chernobyl for days.

FIRST REACTIONS

A 40-year-old Muscovite only learned in conversation with foreigners that leaking radioactivity from Chernobyl had crossed the borders of the Soviet Union. Her reaction:

"My God, – and I thought it was just a local disaster!"

Many Soviet citizens are skeptical about their own media. But the absent news about Chernobyl did not cause panic or major rumors. On the contrary:

A limited accident, in which even the dead and wounded are admitted, is considered credible. The time and cause of catastrophes are usually kept secret by the state press for a long time anyway. Even the cautious information policy in the case of Chernobyl did not arouse excessive mistrust.

In addition, the Soviet public is not aware of any critical debate about nuclear energy. If there is any harmful use of nuclear power at all, so the propaganda tenor goes, then this is done by greedy monopolies in capitalist countries. An essay on deficiencies in nuclear power plants, as it had just been published in a Soviet magazine warning about Chernobyl before the accident, is one of the major exceptions.

The significance of a radioactive accident in a nuclear power plant is therefore less spectacular for most Soviet citizens than one of the frequent earthquakes in the Central Asian republics.

An exception, however, are those who listen to western radio stations: Informed via BBC London, the VoA (Voice of America) or DW (Deutsche Welle), such listeners occasionally turn to foreigners in Moscow for further information.

In this way, despite the May holidays, the first rumors seem to be spreading. A ward doctor in a Moscow infectious disease clinic urgently advised on request to wash or peel all fruit. "Preferably," said another man in Moscow, "one should inquire now at the markets whether goods from Ukraine are being sold."

At the end of last week, schoolchildren in Moscow had allegedly been asked to take great care in dealing with fruit because of the risk of rat poisoning. "But so far", according to medical experts, "there is no special information concerning health issues."

Now, even products from Poland can hardly be sold on Western markets because of the feared contamination. The reaction by a resigned Soviet citizen was: "Then, probably we will end up buying these things from Poland."

CRITICISM OF THE WEST

On Soviet television, the Moscow engineer F. A. Shvets described his reaction to Western depictions of the Chernobyl nuclear power plant accident as a "feeling of bitterness". He compared the accident with the Challenger disaster[34], which caused mourning among the Soviet population; while the West in face of Chernobyl shows no sympathy, but judges on the principle of "the worse the better". Where the engineer got his detailed knowledge of Western media from, however, remained unclear.

The only witnesses of a so called exaggerated fear campaign in the West were British tourists; they had complained in the main Soviet television news program that they were being persuaded to return home from the Soviet Union because of horror reports in Britain of a nuclear catastrophe.

British guest scientists, who were recalled from Kiev, were outraged, speaking to Soviet journalists, that they had been forced to have their clothes checked for radioactivity before departure and to exchange them for sport suits. When the flight director of the British plane then banned the Soviet camera team from entering the plane and even interrupted the interviews, the otherwise rather monotonous TV news program *Vremya* had its scandal.

"Even these foreigners," interpreted the retiree A. G. Kaplyug the following day on television the statements of the British scientists, "understand as well as we do that the

---

[34] The Space Shuttle Challenger disaster was an incident in the US space program on January 28, 1986. Challenger broke apart 73 seconds after take-off, killing all seven crew members aboard.

Western attitude to Chernobyl is pure provocation". The controlled popular anger in the media, however, is countered by the astonishing indifference of many Soviet citizens. They are often skeptical about their own media. But the sparse news flow of the first week has caused neither panic nor major rumors. On the contrary.

Such a limited industrial accident is all the more credible among Soviet citizens, because even officially dead and wounded were reported. Moreover, the reassuring affirmations that a state commission with experts had been set up freed many Soviet citizens – accustomed to authority – from further worries.

In the case of Chernobyl, the formulaic language of the typical reports of catastrophes has avoided speaking of fraternal help from all the republics of the Soviet Union. This, too, according to the customary opinion in the country, testifies to a situation whose consequences have been mastered by the state authorities.

Moreover, Soviet citizens are used to the fact that the time and cause of a disaster are usually kept secret for a long time. It is only after a certain time interval that the media occasionally surprises the public with a detailed report – be it on space travel, environmental damage or an earthquake.

The state media avoid the spectacular moment to report live on site. In the case of Chernobyl, however, the Soviet public is not aware of any critical debate about nuclear energy. If there is any harmful use of nuclear power at all, according to the tenor of earlier propaganda, then it is being done by greedy monopolies in capitalist countries. Essays on deficiencies in nuclear power plants, as recently published in a Soviet magazine, warning about Chernobyl, are rather the exception. On the other hand, television reports and glossy brochures proudly propagate nuclear power as a clean and safe source of energy.

Soviet citizens who listen to foreign radio stations from the West are an exception in this closed information circle. Despite the May holidays in the Soviet capital, rumors seem to have spread in this way.

Foreign correspondents, who wanted to interview arriving passengers at the Kiev railway station in Moscow, were pushed aside by "civilian" gentlemen. The station police were also prepared for the foreign questioners:

"Instead of spreading panic here," said one uniformed man, "you should rather report on the nuclear danger of the US missiles at your place in Western Europe."

FIRST FILM REPORT
ON TELEVISION

A helicopter flies over Chernobyl and shows some blurred footage of the scene of the catastrophe – then a panning over the surrounding settlement with dozens of high buildings. Some trucks can be spotted on a large access road. Otherwise there is no one to be seen. Also the pictures from the exterior of the power plant itself, which were taken from the ground, do not give a reliable impression, because the Soviet camera only glides past concrete walls as high as a man. Soviet television wants to prove with this first film report that the buildings in Chernobyl did not suffer any major destruction, as allegedly claimed in the West.

But instead of publishing real information about the time, cause and course of the disaster, the Soviet media launched a press campaign with the motto: Attack is the best defense. The reactions in Western countries are dismissed as "slander" and "provocation". In front of the television cameras of state journalists, Soviet citizens express feelings of bitterness and indignation at the shame allegedly inflicted on them by the foreign media.

The news that some countries are refusing to import Soviet products evokes in some ways a kind of patriotic defiance among Soviet citizens. The controlled popular anger in the media, however, does not answer the question of where the cited Soviet citizens got their knowledge of Western representations from, having only access to limited information inside the Soviet Union. The highlight of this press campaign has been a TASS commentary, which has turned into an absurd picture.

Literal quotation: "In earlier times ... a decent man would have put a bullet through his head to save his honor... He would have found himself in a similar situation to that in which some Western politicians today find themselves, who are describing the so-called horrors and the allegedly devastating consequences of Chernobyl. ... But so far no suicides have been reported from Western capitals to save political prestige."

This, according to TASS in the original text.

The bitter language reveals how deeply those responsible in the Soviet Union have been affected. Nevertheless, even in today's issue of *Pravda* there is no sign of any willingness to recognize the fine distinction between cause and effect. In euphemistic words, *Pravda* says that the Soviet Union informed the governments of many countries as well as international organizations and societies about the accident. The criticism of Moscow is limited to voices from the USA and NATO allies. The fact that even socialist brother states had taken precautions against radioactive contamination has so far gone unmentioned.

Meanwhile, reports in the media about normal collective farm life, cheering May celebrations or cycling races in Ukraine, have taken on an unusual dimension. In front of the camera the farmer reaches into the fertile and – as should be signaled – unpolluted farmland; in the meadows the first daisies bloom and dance groups enjoy themselves in folk costumes under a blue sky.

Those who still have doubts about the harmlessness of Chernobyl will be convinced by the trip of Prime Minister Ryzhkov to the disaster area. The wording in the press that Nikolai Ryzhkov and his Politburo colleague Yegor Ligachyov visited people who had been temporarily evacuated is also intended to show Soviet citizens that everything will be in order in the foreseeable future.

May 6, 1986

LETTER OF THE WEST GERMAN AMBASSADOR IN MOSCOW
(I)

THE AMBASSADOR
OF THE FEDERAL REPUBLIC OF GERMANY

Moscow, May 6, 1986

To the
Members of the
German Colony

Dear Compatriots!

The reactor accident in Chernobyl (Ukrainian SSR) worries us all understandably very much. Unfortunately, despite constant requests, the Soviet authorities have not yet contributed to dispersing this unrest through their restrictive information policy. The information on the possible consequences of the accident is still far from sufficient. The Embassy of the Federal Republic of Germany is therefore largely dependent on its own investigations. Our own measurements, which we carried out in Moscow in the last few days, showed values in the normal range and still give no cause for concern. The general weather situation which prevailed in the European part of the USSR last week also led to radioactive dust being transported more to the north-northwest, west and southwest of the USSR and the Moscow area having been largely spared from this so far.

On the basis of the information currently available to us, I see no reason to make any particular recommendations to you here in Moscow.

As far as food consumption is concerned, after a discussion on May 5, 1986 between the agricultural officers of the American, Dutch, Swedish and our embassies (all four are professional farmers with many years of experience in the Soviet Union and intimately familiar with the situation), the situation was as follows.

<u>Dairy products:</u>

For practical reasons and because of their perishability, fresh milk and other dairy products consumed in Moscow are also produced in Moscow and not imported from Ukraine.

<u>Meat products:</u>

If radioactive fallout is deposited on the soil, it takes several weeks before it can also be measured in meat or meat products.

The meat consumed in Moscow also comes largely from the Moscow region.

<u>Vegetables and fruit:</u>

The products currently offered in shops or collective farm markets are either from last year's harvest or produced in greenhouses. Contamination by radioactivity can be largely ruled out here. However, thorough washing or removal of the peel is recommended.

<u>*Water:*</u>
Moscow's water supply comes from the north and northeast of the city. When the water is treated, it passes through filter systems that retain suspended matter and reduce radioactive contamination to a minimum.

In the last few days, a team of experts from the USA has already carried out measurements on a number of food products which have not yet been completed but which have not yet shown increased values.

There are therefore no concerns about the consumption of food purchased in Moscow. This is the current situation.

We cannot yet answer the question of whether crops harvested from mid-June, such as vegetables, berries, cereals and sugar beets, will be contaminated.

However, the embassy will pursue this question together with other Western representations and I will inform you of the outcome in due course.

With a friendly greeting,

Your,
(Jörg Kastl)

THE TIME OF THE EXPLOSION

The representatives from Great Britain living in Moscow have fresh milk flown in from London as a precaution, while the American embassy reassures its compatriots by saying that there is no cause for concern in the Soviet capital. Nevertheless, American citizens in Moscow also order their milk from Finland.

In this contradictory situation, the Soviet press has provided further information on the Chernobyl accident with a number of, sometimes detailed, reports. From this, Soviet citizens can deduce not only the exact time of the accident, but also the possible extent of the evacuation measures.

The picture is as follows:

In the night in question from Friday, April 25 to Saturday, April 26, the explosion must have occurred.[35] The first measures were taken by the night watchmen, who are described by the party newspaper *Pravda* as "lieutenants". The first evacuation operation is said to have lasted about four hours, during which the approximately 25,000 residents and employees from the immediate vicinity of the nuclear power plant were brought to safety.[36] However, it remains unclear what intensity of radiation these people were exposed to. Similarly, it is not clear that the fire that broke out in the reactor has actually been extinguished. Rather, it is said that an

---

[35] The exact time was April 26, 1986, 01:23:48 a.m. Moscow time. Cf. p. 13.

[36] It does not say when the evacuation started, but only that it took four hours. According to *Pravda* later on, the evacuation of the affected population began only 36 hours after the accident. Cf. p. 62.

unusually difficult situation has arisen, since the fire cannot be fought with water or with any chemicals.

What is striking about this latest presentation is the fact that there is still talk of a complicated situation and that air measurements have included other major cities besides Kiev.

Another newspaper report today literally asserts:

"If there is even the slightest doubt about the quality of products, it will not be sold." In the affected regions, milk, fruit and other products would be tested for possible contamination before and after transport.

Meanwhile, Soviet television has broadcasted street interviews from Kiev: The aim was to show that, contrary to Western claims, there was no panic and that there could be no talk of thousands of deaths.

However, it was publicly announced that Dr. Robert Gale, an American specialist for bone marrow, had come to the country at the invitation of the Soviet Union. Also, the many thanks to named doctors in the disaster area show that the medical consequences of the accident must be considerable.

May 6, 1986

MORE QUESTIONS
THAN ANSWERS

Why did the Soviet Union once again hesitate so long in the event of a disaster before going public with the necessary information?

This question cannot be answered even after the first press conference on Chernobyl in Moscow.

Of course, concrete information is now available: the time of the accident is officially mentioned. This is a confirmation for everyone outside the country who had already suspected the night from Friday to Saturday in the last week of April as the date of the accident, on the basis of measurement data.

Only the "sensationalist greed of the Western media" – as the Soviet Union sees it – secretly expects even more deaths. Indeed, the known victims are already bad enough. And Moscow is not afraid to call for medical help in America for the worst affected cases.

The gratitude of the Soviet public towards the foreign doctors who have now arrived in Moscow is sincere. Just as sincere is the dismay of the Soviet people over what has happened. But unsatisfactory is the fact that the cause of the accident still remains in the dark.

Is the Soviet Union not willing or not able to provide any information here?

It sounds very daring to talk about a series of peripheral, insignificant and therefore unforeseeable coincidences, all of which have contributed to this disaster. With this information, perhaps a few hundred journalists can be put off in the brevity of the one-hour press conference. But what about the state and party leadership itself?

They obviously need more specific information. And furthermore: Figures alone do not clarify the extent of the disaster among those affected. One has to interpret the daily press and the statements of those responsible separately to recognize that at least 25,000 people were exposed to the intense radiation for a minimum of ten to twelve hours, which according to Soviet data amounted to 15 millirem per hour.[37]

The evacuation of the residents from the immediate vicinity – it was now made clear – could not be completed until the afternoon of the following day.

It would be foolish to speculate here with the misfortune of the Soviet people. But it is just as foolish on the Soviet side not to do everything to prevent such speculations from arising in the first place.

At this moment, however, the Moscow leadership points to the local authorities at the site. Allegedly, the gravity of the disaster had not been correctly assessed. Throughout the incident, there were constant breakdowns in the chain-of-information. And finally, the members of the investigation commission were thousands of miles apart. All this – so the excuse – takes time.

Must it really have to be like that in a nuclear disaster?

Typically, in the case of similar breakdowns elsewhere, surely people would like to put the blame on someone else.

At the same moment, however, the Moscow gentlemen of ministerial rank made their commitment to the further and accelerated expansion of nuclear energy. Andranik Petrosyants, head of the Soviet nuclear energy authority, spoke of the fact that no country is better or worse when it comes to technology and the use of nuclear power.

The solidarity of the experts superimposes political dissonances, which used to accuse the evil capitalistic class

---

[37] IAEA stated 36 millirem a few days later. Cf. p. 60.

enemy of using nuclear power recklessly and against the interests of the people. Therefore, at this press conference the Soviets didn't miss presenting a simultaneous call for nuclear disarmament.

But even the Foreign Ministry, which was responsible for this press conference, did not want to make room for such a political range. One hour was enough for only one performance, which contained enough reassuring, if not very informative, statements to be shown to the Soviet public on television tonight.

The West is waiting for further insights.

HEAD OF IAEA
CORRECTS MOSCOW

The Soviet Union has committed itself to regular monitoring of radioactivity along its western border and in the area about 40 miles southeast of the Chernobyl accident site. The data, which are determined under the same conditions and at the same time, are made available to the International Atomic Energy Agency in Vienna.

This consequence of the nuclear accident was announced today at a press conference held in Moscow by the Director General of the International Atomic Energy Agency (IAEA), Hans Blix. However, the experts who travelled to Moscow were unable to find out the final cause of the Chernobyl accident. Obviously, the Soviet authorities do not yet have a sufficient overview of the disaster to be able to provide more precise information than before. At a conference later this year, however, all the investigative material will be evaluated.

At this press conference, the Swede Hans Blix essentially described once again the Soviet presentation of the course of events of the accident. In individual points, however, differences were noticeable. Today it was said that the highest radioactivity measured in the night of the accident was 36 millirem[38] per hour. So far, Soviet sources had only spoken of 10 to 15 millirem.

---

[38] Since Germany was especially hit by the nuclear fallout of Chernobyl I quote the official limits by German standards: "The limit value for the effective dose for the protection of individuals of the population in Germany is 1 millisievert (= 10 millirem) per calendar year. The radiation exposure from a single nuclear plant via the waste water and exhaust air exposure pathways must not exceed 0.3 millisievert (= 3 millirem) per

At the same time, it was made clear that Moscow did not inform the nuclear energy authority IAEA in Vienna of the nuclear accident on its own initiative. Only at Sweden's request about increased radioactivity – according to Hans Blix – did the IAEA turn to the Soviet representatives in Vienna, who in turn had asked Moscow for a statement. Further facts were clarified at this press conference: The Soviet Union did not shut down nuclear reactors of the same type, as assumed in the West. Meanwhile, small amounts of radioactivity continue to escape from Chernobyl. However, the source of the fire should eventually be extinguished. Nevertheless, the experts from Vienna could not rule out the possibility that an actual physical melting through of the reactor could not be prevented. But the Soviet side claims that the temperature in the reactor is far lower than required for such a melting process.

Only indirectly did the neutral observers from Vienna, including one American, conclude that they might have expected more information. It was literally said that the Soviet side could not present a systematic list of radioactive measurements. However, the Viennese emissaries warned against any hysteria or exaggerated fear.

From the Ukrainian capital Kiev, where they had spent several hours on the streets, they described normal life, no panic, and no immediate danger to people's health.

---

year.". (§§ 46, 47 of the German Radiation Protection Ordinance). Retrieved August 5, 2019 under
https://www.bfs.de/DE/themen/ion/strahlenschutz/grenzwerte/grenzwerte.html
For the English definition retrieved June 11, 2020 under
https://en.wikipedia.org/wiki/Roentgen_equivalent_man

CRITICISM AND REVERSAL
OF THE INFORMATION POLICY

The Soviet Union's information policy on the nuclear accident did not only frighten the Western public. Critique came also from inside the Soviet Union. An important advisor to the top leadership, Georgy Arbatov, head of the Moscow Institute for USA and Canada Studies, called this policy literally a sin. And also the party newspaper *Pravda* criticized this form of information policy. Sufficient cadres of leaders in the Kremlin's sphere of influence have noticed how much the reputation of the Soviet Union has suffered internationally.

The obvious conclusion is that everything that Mr. Gorbachev himself signals as confidence-building measures or disarmament proposals, as offers of control or readiness to talk, is now dismissed as untrustworthy. In the first angry reactions to the disaster, these conclusions have probably emerged in many countries. For many observers Moscow is a place of concealment. If the Soviet side is to be set on accuracy, the statements made by Hans Blix, the Director General of the International Atomic Energy Agency, also offer illustrative material for new irritations:

– It was not Moscow, for its part, that informed the IAEA about Chernobyl, but Moscow only responded to an anxious demand.

– Not only 10-15 millirem of radiation escaped per hour in the night of the accident in question, but 36 millirem.

– The evacuation of the population did not begin as early as the next morning, as *Pravda* showed, but only 36 hours after the accident.

All these grave differences concerning information can no longer be attributed to subordinates who did not adequately inform their headquarters in Moscow. For at least a week, the government and party bodies in Moscow tried to save face, even at the expense of the whole truth.

Now the turnaround has begun: The truth should be on the table. Such demands fit in with Lenin's relevant quotations, which are back in business under Gorbachev. But which institutions are uniting a realistic description of the situation? Is this "someone" perhaps the secretary general himself, who does not speak when the most serious nuclear accident to date breaks out, when he otherwise likes to present himself to the citizens in a populist manner?

One might rightly ask why Gorbachev himself is silent and why a dispute about the right information policy breaks out at the lower levels of power? Gorbachev's vertical take-off in the Western media almost ended in a nosedive. But this is where the Soviet Union and Mr. Gorbachev himself probably are being done an injustice. The Soviet Union and its head are unsure of themselves. The description of "a tragic accident" is more than an understatement for what is happening in Chernobyl. How must Mikhail Gorbachev feel during all this, when he knows so much more through his informants than the remaining 280 million citizens of his country? It would be time now for him to sit in front of the television camera and explain that closer cooperation and trust are necessary – not despite, but precisely because of a disaster that also affects foreign countries.

Mr. Gorbachev's far-reaching disarmament plans, with their verbal guidelines, could be confirmed at this point with a policy of genuine openness. Otherwise we will be left with the suspicion that everything, absolutely everything, that comes out of the Soviet Union, is just empty words.

WHAT HAS HAPPENED
SO FAR

It all began for the Soviet citizens with a mere four-line and rather inconspicuous first TASS message: An accident somewhere in the Ukraine. A state commission is already taking care of it. Only a few people were alarmed by the fact that the accident had happened in a nuclear power plant. Even less worrisome for most was the wording that a certain amount of radioactivity had leaked. The news language of the official agency TASS was limited to a stereotyped reassurance.

If this had been the only message, no one in the Soviet Union would have been particularly upset. At best, some clever comrades might have said: Look here, a sign of our new openness, that even now we announce such accidents in our own country. But all this would have been possible only if the disaster had happened somewhere in the heart of Siberia, not on the border with neighboring countries.

But then another communication soon followed from the Council of Ministers. There was a second statement, mentioning deaths and injuries. Nevertheless, panic did not break out in the country. The media confined itself to repeating this second statement. No further comment was made. And now something began that is difficult for Western citizens to understand:

Many Soviet people now actually believed in greater openness in the field of information: for the dead and injured – so the argument of many – were not so easily admitted in the past.

What was already recorded outside the country's borders as a minus point for the Soviet leadership, namely delayed and insufficient information about the catastrophe, that only moved a small percentage of people within the Soviet Union.

Only those Soviet citizens who were informed by Western radio stations suddenly pricked up their ears. The irony of the story: On the same day when TASS spread its first report about Chernobyl, the Soviet Foreign Ministry had invited the foreign correspondents accredited in Moscow to a press conference. It was about the alleged propaganda of Western radio stations interfering in the internal affairs of Soviet power. The chief witness to this event was the previous deputy editor-in-chief of the Russian program of Radio Liberty in Munich. From this station, which was operated and financed by the USA, a certain Oleg Tumanov had returned to the Soviet Union via unknown paths after twenty years of exile in the West. Now he sat there, talking of lies and propaganda, and no one could suspect that, like a boomerang, his accusations would be vividly made only hours later in the same office responsible for this event.

For on the afternoon of the same day, the Swedish ambassador contacted the Ministry of Foreign Affairs in Moscow. His urgent request: He demanded clarification about a radioactive cloud coming from the Soviet Union, which had passed over Sweden. The Moscow authorities' response was negative, although it would not have taken much effort to ask at least once at the information department of the Central Committee or at TASS.

The first declaration on Chernobyl was being prepared there, which was to be issued only a few hours after the Swedish request. The ambassador had to leave without having achieved anything and afterwards felt betrayed, even lied to, by the Soviet Foreign Ministry.

The back and forth between East and West for initial information finally reached the International Atomic Energy Agency in Vienna. Only after a request from Vienna did the Soviets admit that there had been an accident in which radioactivity had been released. No data on the quantity, no information on possible or suspected causes were given. No data on the fight against the consequences. Of course, Moscow's later assertion that the International Atomic Energy Agency had been informed in Vienna was correct. But not on Moscow's own initiative, as the world public should be made to believe.

The general director of the IAEA himself, the Swede Hans Blix, made it clear, that it was the other way around. Only two weeks after the explosion, Blix had travelled to the scene of the accident at the invitation of the Soviet government. In Moscow he told the international press about the fact, that the Soviet Union did not actively inform the IAEA right after the disaster.

Meanwhile, a dispute had already broken out in the Soviet hierarchy over information policy in view of the biggest nuclear accident to date. A press conference by the responsible politicians was rather disappointing. Soviet reports from the Ukraine sounded contradictory.

On television in the evening the dairy cows grazed, the farmer walked through the brown field and praised the fertility of the Ukrainian soil. Meanwhile, a TASS correspondent reported that special trains and planes were being used to bring the children of the evacuated areas away from Kiev as well. In the Ukrainian capital itself, people were supposed to line up in front of the ticket counters. Many wanted to leave the catchment area of the danger zone. Word had gradually spread that radioactivity could not be compared to the dust of a coal-fired power station.

Finally, in *Pravda* was written of the sin of a false information policy. Those responsible had realized what a setback they themselves had inflicted on the country. Since then, the number of reports from the disaster area has increased.

Recommendations that children should not play on the streets and that windows should not be opened for more than an hour, calls on the radio to be careful with fruit and vegetables, all this has now been publicly acknowledged. The fact that the Viennese envoys of the Atomic Energy Agency also received far higher radioactivity data from official sources than the Soviet Union had previously stated is evidence of a rethinking on the part of the responsible politicians. Measuring stations are now being set up to monitor the emission of radioactivity along the western border areas. The measurement data can be evaluated internationally.

After two weeks of hesitation, Moscow has finally admitted that the reactor accident in Chernobyl is not an internal affair of the Soviet Union.

May 11, 1986

REASSURANCE CAMPAIGN
OF THE MEDIA

The saleswoman in a Moscow bread shop, which is also open on Sundays, does not want to comment on Chernobyl. She refers to the television news from the evening before: "You could see for yourself," she argues in her white sales dress, "how people drank water and fished. Everything near Chernobyl! Or do you think the camera is lying or the doctors are lying?"

In fact, the Soviet media did not use politicians in their calming campaign, but experts, especially doctors, to carry out and explain their test measurements in front of the camera.

The result is always the same: No danger to the people's health. Should there really be concern among the population or people who want to leave the scene of the accident, then at least they cannot be identified in Soviet reporting. But even at the Kiev railway station in downtown Moscow, two weeks after the accident, there are no excited crowds of people fleeing Ukraine with emergency luggage. There are more trains arriving than planned in the timetable. But there is no panic, horror or fear among the passengers. They tend to react with rejection to questions. The May holidays are imminent, the big holidays. They want to take the children to their grandparents in the countryside. However, a striking number of children are said to have already arrived in Moscow from Ukraine.

Only among close friends do rumors circulate with horror numbers of dead and wounded. But as soon as someone should name the source of his knowledge, many remain silent. They are just rumors. Or one refers to acquaintances of relatives, who in turn would have phoned friends of friends in

Kiev. Verifiable information – so it would seem – is also hardly to be received. Nevertheless, Soviet citizens can participate indirectly in the Chernobyl drama. The government newspaper *Izvestia* published a report from a hospital in which some of the most severely contaminated victims are housed. Most of them are firefighters who were deployed in the reactor to fight the fire and did not yet know anything about the radioactivity. The heroic efforts of these people must have been followed by a frightened reaction from the nursing staff. Many were not prepared to deal with such radiation victims. Allegedly, even specially ordered soldiers took on the task of stripping the contaminated victims when they were admitted.

After these two weeks, it is difficult to assess the real mood in the country. Despite the Chernobyl disaster, the people were busy with important Soviet May holidays. And now that the scale of the disaster seems to be visible even to poorly informed Soviet citizens, two completely different reactions can be observed: An almost incomprehensible patriotism in this matter leads to the catastrophe being played down as much as possible and occasionally equated with American nuclear tests.

Other Soviet citizens, on the other hand, deny their leadership any credibility and, against their better judgement, draw a horror picture of the scene of the disaster. What is striking, however, is that astonishingly many Soviet people wonder why party leader Gorbachev himself did not travel to Chernobyl, when he had otherwise so often come to other regions and found himself ready to chat with people on the street. But at the very least they expect the Kremlin leader to finally appear on television in the near future and to comment on Chernobyl and the consequences of the catastrophe.

May 12, 1986

LETTER OF THE WEST GERMAN AMBASSADOR IN MOSCOW
(II)

THE AMBASSADOR
OF THE FEDERAL REPUBLIC OF GERMANY

Moscow, May 12, 1986

To the
Members of the
German Colony

Dear Compatriots!

The staff of the Embassy of the Federal Republic of Germany in Moscow still feel obliged to inform and advise you and your relatives about the situation after the reactor accident in Chernobyl.

In all our measurements and investigations, which we carried out last week also with food from the collective farm market, we could not determine any increased or even dangerous radiation values. We exchange our experiences and data daily with measurements of other Western representatives. At present, an American team of specialists is in Moscow to carry out air and water measurements and to examine foodstuffs. The Embassy and other foreign representatives sent food and water samples to their respective home countries for laboratory testing. These tests, too, have so far yielded no radiation values that are hazardous to health anywhere.

None of the Western representations has therefore so far considered it necessary to fly in food from abroad or to order such steps. Deliveries of food (milk) in the last 2 weeks, which e.g. British and Americans ordered, were not a result of the accident, but were orders like these colony members make regularly – even before Chernobyl.

Tonight, 05.12.1986, a specialist from Germany will come to Moscow, who will take special care of the quality of food from local shops and kolkhoz markets and who will carry out further measurements with a special device.

You will also have the opportunity to have your food purchased in Moscow inspected at the embassy if you have any doubts about its purity.

Further samples and a larger number of measurements can give us a reliable overview of the quality of the goods.

Since it cannot be said with absolute certainty that goods from the Ukraine will not reach the collective farm markets – contrary to official assurances – you are at liberty to obtain supplies from the Beryozka shops.[39] However, neither these nor other Western embassies see any current reason to do so.

With a friendly greeting,
Your,
(Jörg Kastl)

---

[39] Special shops in the Soviet Union in which rare Soviet products and Western goods were sold for hard currency.

FIRST TV REPORT ON SITE

Slowly the car rolls towards the roadblock. A policeman with a mask opens the barrier. Through the windshield, the television camera detects abandoned villages and covered-up wells. No one on the street, no cattle on the pasture.

These first pictures from the restricted area thirty kilometers (eighteen miles) around Chernobyl were broadcast on Soviet television.

Then the Soviet TV journalist visited the task force to combat the consequences of the accident. "Until Sunday the possibility of a catastrophe had existed", reported the totally exhausted nuclear scientist Yevgeny Velikhov in front of the camera. "This danger is now over." But what kind of catastrophe could have occurred could not be clarified the next day in a press conference with the spokesman of the foreign office Vladimir Lomeiko.

Instead, the party newspaper *Pravda* published another report on the scene of the disaster and surprised with sharp attacks on the cadre of leaders, named by name, who had acted wrongly in the catastrophe situation. Occasionally the evacuees were not even given clothes and their justified requests were ignored. The chief engineer Shapoval for instance reacted with – literally – "complete indifference" to the fate of the evacuated people. *Pravda* accuses some of those responsible of "political immaturity, inactivity and incomprehension". The aforementioned Shapoval had already been excluded from the ranks of the Communist Party. At the same time, the concern among the population should be counteracted.

The same report promises that the *Pravda* correspondents will meet the evacuees again as soon as they return to their old homes near the nuclear power plant.

This raises the hope that no totally hopeless situation can have arisen in the immediate vicinity of Chernobyl. Finally, the newspaper reports that the grain harvest is being prepared just outside the forbidden zone on the collective farms. The milk of cows fed on green fodder is also in use. But the most important part of this calming campaign is dedicated to water.

For example, the TV news program *Vremya* showed nearby Ukrainian health resorts where guests drank mineral water directly from the spring. At the same time, however, those responsible assure that – if radioactivity were actually to enter the drinking water reservoir of the Ukrainian capital Kiev, there would be other ways of supplying the two and a half million inhabitants of the city without any problems.

Райком работает круглые сутки

Чернобыльская АЭС: проверка на мужество

О чём я мечтаю? — переспросил мастер электроцеха АЭС В. Лыскин. — О том времени, когда мы вернёмся в Припять, начнём нормально жить и работать. Знаю, что такое придёт, но для этого нужно работать для себя... И давайте так договоримся: всё будет позади, вы проведёте читательскую конференцию «Правды» в нашем Доме культуры. Согласны? «Правда» принимает это предложение.

В очерках, корреспонденциях, репортажах мы будем рассказывать о ходе ликвидации аварии на Чернобыльской АЭС, о героических трудовых буднях как на промплощадке, так и в районах, где сейчас находятся жители из эвакуированной зоны. А потом, когда жители Припяти вернутся домой и станция начнёт нормально работать, выездная бригада «Правды» проведёт читательскую конференцию на АЭС.

...не такое заседание бюро партии длилось бы, надо полагать, дольше и говорилось бы, очевидно, больше. Сейчас на долгие разговоры нет, минута нелегка, и дорога каждая минута. Прошло десять того момента, как коллектив Чернобыльского филиала отраслевого производственного объединения «Южатомэнерго» эвакуировался в составе более 200 человек вместе с жителями Полесского и Иванковского районов. Однако за это время руководители А. Шаповал и А. Сичкаренко ничего не сделали для находящихся в их ведении людей, обеспечения их ра... была выдана своевременно зарплата, не выделена... игнорировались законные просьбы эвакуированных.

...Из 18 коммунистов Припятского управления сейчас только двое остались в строю, остальные на обследовании в больницах, — рассказывает первый секретарь горкома партии А. Гаманюк. — Но такая обстановка ещё более сплачивает, организовывает людей.

Кстати, самого секретаря горкома весть об аварии застала в больнице. Александр Сергеевич тут же оставил больничную койку и возглавил работу партийного комитета.

— Заседания бюро райкома стали короче, но они проводятся чаще. Этого требует оперативная обстановка, — говорит секретарь. — Сейчас многие коллективы предприятий и организаций Припяти разместились в Полесском районе. Эвакуация проводилась в сжатые сроки, и некоторые подразделения оказались как бы расчленёнными, а люди разделёнными. За первые десять дней мая хозяйственные руководители уточнили и решают сейчас проблемы, связанные с перемещением личным составом предприятий и организаций, с временным трудоустройством людей, их очередными отпусками.

В эти дни в каждом из хозяйств проходят открытые партийные собрания на которых обсуждаются задачи коммунистов, партийных организаций по усилению массово-политической работы, организованному проведению подготовки и уборке урожая нынешнего года и его заготовке.

В совхозе «Хабне», где проводил собрание первый секретарь Полесского райкома партии ...атомэнергостройтранса», исключительные случаи. На этом же заседании бюро горкома партии приводились многочисленные факты самоотверженного, мужественного поведения руководителей-коммунистов, сумевших в трудной обстановке проявить высокие организаторские качества, личную смелость. Называли прежде всего имена А. Нагородного и В. Дейграфа из Чернобыльского монтажного управления, Н. Скляреца и В. Абрамова из припятского управления «Южтеплоэнергомонтаже». Следуя примеру своих вожаков, решительно действовали и члены их коллективов.

менных партийных групп, а также партийные группы в вахтенных сменах на Чернобыльской АЭС. Их усилия направлены на мобилизацию трудящихся по ликвидации последствий аварии.

Припятский горком партии находится временно в помещении Полесского райкома Компартии Украины, и действуют обе партийные организации сейчас в тесном контакте. Самая дружеская деловая связь установлена в работе партийной организации колхоза имени 40-летия Октября и прибывших сюда с АЭС коммунистов. Их оказалось тринадцать. Парторгом они избрали С. Родионова — заместителя секретаря партийной организации управления «Южэнергомонтажвентиляция». На совместном заседании партбюро были намечены меры организационного порядка, связанные с налаживанием быта, организацией трудоустройства прибывших. И вот уже электросварщик В. Новохатский занялся ремонтом колхозной техники, А. Горбунов — рабочий с АЭС вышел с колхозной бригадой на возведение закрытого сенохранилища. Их здесь сооружают два.

— Всем работы хватит, — говорит бригадир строительной бригады колхоза комсомолец Сергей Степанчук.

В Полесском районе тринадцать хозяйств. При каждом из них работают штабы по обеспечению нормальных условий труда и жизни эвакуированных. В состав штабов входят представители партийных организаций как бригад, прибывших из Припяти, так и местных колхозов.

Н. Приймаченко, уже начали косить рапс для закладки раннего силоса. Его надо заготовить 800 тонн. Механизаторы заблаговременно отремонтировали здесь агрегаты для приготовления витаминной муки. Животноводы совхоза умело используют зелёный корм, идущий сейчас с угодий хозяйства — например, на молочнотоварной ферме, возглавляемой делегатом XXVII съезда Компартии Украины Ниной Савченко, увеличили в мае суточные надои молока на каждую корову но сравнению с тем же периодом прошлого года на один килограмм 200 граммов.

Понимая, что ликвидация последствий аварии на АЭС в Чернобыле требует от каждого удвоения, утроения усилий, животноводы совхоза «Владимирский» выступили с предложением, пересмотреть ранее взятые обязательства на 1986 год и получить от каждой коровы по три тысячи килограммов молока. Полесский райком партии одобрил патриотический почин, который получил уже на фермах района широкое распространение.

Бывая в эти дни в районных комитетах партии в Киевской области, мы наблюдали сосредоточенную, продуманную работу их инструкторов, заведующих отделами, секретарей. Чётко, без спешки, оперативно решаются трудные проблемы. Всюду заметны конкретность и деловитость в каждом шаге партийных работников, отсутствие лишних слов, туманных обещаний.

— В этих условиях, — сказал первый секретарь Припятского горкома партии А. Гаманюк, — мы не имеем права позволить себе никакого расслабления. Время рассчитано буквально по минутам, хотя партийный комитет работает почти круглые сутки. Решение кратче и точнее, выполнение быстрое и аккуратное. Обстановка в течение дня и ночи может меняться неоднократно, и каждый раз надо быть готовым к тому, чтобы успеть мобилизовать коммунистов, горячим словом увлечь людей на преодоление трудностей. И ещё для нас очень важно — добиться, чтобы в этих нелёгких условиях, когда всё переместилось, но ещё не осело полностью, не устоялось, коллектив каждого предприятия нашёл своё место, определил свою линию действий. Здесь, конечно, многое зависит сейчас от руководителей, их инициативы, распорядительности, умения и смелости принять самостоятельное, подчас даже рискованное решение, но единственно правильное в данной ситуации. Поэтому на первом месте, впрочем, как и всегда у нас, работа с кадрами...

...Двери в Полесский райком партии не закрываются ни днём, ни ночью. Люди идут и идут сюда за решением самых насущных, самых животрепещущих вопросов.

**В. ГУБАРЕВ,
М. ОДИНЕЦ.**
(Спец. корр. «Правды»).
Киевская область.

На снимке: Чернобыльская АЭС сегодня. Стрелкой показан четвёртый энергоблок станции, на котором произошла авария.

Фото Л. Зуфарова и В. Репика (ТАСС).

"The regional Party Committee is working round-the-clock.
The Chernobyl Nuclear Power Plant: Test of Courage."
Pravda article on Chernobyl, May 12, 1986.

ECONOMIC CONSEQUENCES

More than ninety thousand people had to leave their homes and farms. New housing estates and villages in the Chernobyl restricted area are totally empty. The fields lie fallow. The harvest must be considered as lost. The energy flow of four thousand megawatts from the Chernobyl reactors has dried up. Import restrictions imposed by Western countries and, in the long term, psychological reservations about food from the Soviet Union – all of this is having a negative impact on the economy as a result of the nuclear disaster.

Of course, it is not possible to calculate exactly how much damage the Soviet Union suffers in rubles and kopecks. The evacuees are still promised that they could return to their settlements and villages in the foreseeable future. *Pravda* aroused first hopes when it assured that it would visit the affected people after their return to the decontaminated areas. One day later it was written in the same place that it would take at least months before the disaster area could be used again. So in plain language the signal is given: Be patient, we cannot make any promises.

In addition to social problems that can occur among evacuees in their new environment, there are concrete financial questions. The Politburo has already promised help by decree. But if all belongings had to be lost because of contamination, then the state would have to bear an additional financial burden. All further considerations appear at first glance to be a calculation with several unknowns. Speculations about the real extent of possible grain losses must fail simply because the Soviet Union has not yet published any data showing the extent of soil contamination.

However, there is evidence from Western measurements. In Sweden, for example, emissions of two slowly decomposing substances from the Chernobyl nuclear reactor were detected: cesium and strontium. Both substances pollute the soil for a long time. Therefore, experts expect the full loss of the harvest at least in the immediate vicinity of Chernobyl.

According to cautious projections by Western agricultural experts in Moscow, however, this is hardly likely to be more than 350,000 tons of grain per year. It is not yet clear how many years it will be impossible to use this area for agriculture. According to the American Wharton Institute, the Soviet Union would lose as much as 20 million tons of grain because of Chernobyl. This estimate is obviously wrong: Because, such a quantity presupposes that practically half of Ukraine, which is considered the granary of the Soviet Union, could no longer be used for agricultural purposes. But there are no signs of this from the Soviet point of view.

On the contrary: the party newspaper *Pravda* published a report from the immediate border area of the disaster zone, barely 30 miles from Chernobyl. In almost proud words it describes how diligently the dairy cows there are supplied with fresh green fodder. Also the coming sowing of the fields – according to *Pravda* – is prepared. There is no indication that larger parts of the republic concerned are to be shut down out of caution.

As far as exports abroad are concerned, however, one can be sure that the Soviet Union will examine such products for the smallest radiation doses. Moscow knows that the country's prestige also depends on this. Nevertheless, it would be illusory to believe that Western import restrictions in this sector could hit the Soviet Union hard: Because, the value of food products exported from the Soviet Union as a whole in 1984 – according to the latest available figure – was 1.1 billion rubles, the equivalent of about 3.4 billion German marks. That is only 1.5 percent of total exports. The majority of these exports come from socialist countries, while the West buys only barely more than two hundred million rubles worth of food from the Soviet Union.

What's more, the goods that are now subject to the import ban imposed by the EC (European Community) countries amount to just under 60 million German marks. But even losses in energy supply will not knock over the Soviet Union.

Of course, Chernobyl has in the meantime lost a total output of four thousand megawatts of electricity, most of which has also been used industrially. However, existing coal and hydropower plants in the Ukraine can help to compensate for such losses.

A precise calculation in the energy sector and in the production branches dependent on it is of course difficult. Contrary to earlier reports immediately after the accident, it was not confirmed that the Soviet Union had shut down all reactors of the same type as Chernobyl. The country could also hardly cope with such a power failure, as a good third of all Soviet nuclear power stations would have been affected by such a measure.

Difficulties in oil production also show that the Soviet Union cannot freely resort to raw materials for its own use, a large part of which are exported for hard currency. This is why nuclear power is being expanded even after the Chernobyl disaster. Following the accident, this ambitious program was set up as part of a communiqué between the Soviet Union and the International Atomic Energy Agency in Vienna.

GORBACHEV DEMANDS CONSEQUENCES

As a consequence of the Chernobyl disaster, the Soviet Union is extending its unilateral moratorium on nuclear testing until August 6, 1986, the 40th anniversary of the dropping of the atomic bomb on Hiroshima: Party leader Gorbachev told this to the Soviet television audience at the end of his 25-minute speech. At the same time, he renewed his offer to meet immediately with the American President anywhere in the world – including Hiroshima – to sign an agreement for a definitive ban on nuclear weapons testing.

Gorbachev dedicated the first part of his speech to the events of Chernobyl. In particular, he mentioned the first two deaths from the night of the accident. He also mentioned 299 people who were now hospitalized with radiation sickness. Seven had already died.

According to Gorbachev, the final cause of the accident had not been clarified up till now.

"Now" - so Gorbachev literally - "a work of many years lies before us". The radioactivity is still dangerous for humans.

After thanking countries and people who offered their help, Gorbachev strongly criticized the reaction in some NATO countries and the USA. He accused their governments and representatives of the mass media of an "immoral campaign of rampant Anti-Sovietism". In addition to the US, he particularly criticized the government of the Federal Republic of Germany, which would have seen an opportunity to put obstacles in the way of the East-West dialogue and to justify the arms race.

Gorbachev countered the accusation that the Soviet Union had not provided sufficient information about the Chernobyl accident by saying that it had taken the USA ten days to inform Congress of the Three Mile Island accident in 1979; and even months passed before the world public knew what was going on.

As a result of such accidents, Gorbachev proposed the following four measures:

1. an international security and early warning system with all countries to exchange information with each other immediately;

2. an early conference to be organized by the International Atomic Energy Agency in Vienna on this whole issue;

3. the IAEA's powers should be extended;

4. the UN, the World Health Organization and the UN Environmental program should also be more actively involved to ensure the peaceful use of nuclear energy.

Gorbachev's first TV statement after the disaster, published the next day in *Pravda*, May 15, 1986.

HELP FROM THE USA

The Soviet Union is making sustained efforts to rectify initial deficiencies in the reporting on Chernobyl. These include vivid film reports from the disaster site itself, frank statements by scientists about the severity of the accident and the admission of an even growing number of injured and dead.

This is also the context for today's press conference given by Robert Gale, the American specialist in bone marrow transplantation. Gale had come to the Soviet Union through the mediation of Armand Hammer, a major American industrialist, to work with a team of Moscow doctors on the most serious cases of radioactive contamination.

According to Gale, 19 out of 35 patients with the highest radiation dose received a bone marrow transplant. The remaining patients from this risk group were not eligible for transplantation because they already had too much other organic damage. Seven of these 35 patients had already died. From the information of the American physician one must draw the conclusion that further fatalities are to be expected.

Gale praised the international cooperation: 15 countries had helped with equipment and medicines. Only indirectly did he address the fact that it would have been desirable in individual cases for medicines to be dispatched more quickly. However, according to Gale, the Soviet side had guaranteed all possibilities for smooth work.

Other specialists from the USA and Israel are working with Gale in Moscow. The American industrialist Armand Hammer had personally taken over the financing of all deliveries of medicines and equipment brought to the Soviet Union. The 87-year-old had already fought against hunger and typhus in the Soviet Union as a doctor at the age of 23. He is one of Lenin's few still living interlocutors. As an entrepreneur, Hammer was particularly committed to Soviet-American relations.

At the press conference, neither Gale nor his Soviet colleague Andrei Vorobyov wanted to make any forecasts about the further course of Chernobyl or its possible long-term consequences. However, Vorobyov assured that there was no danger for the people outside the 30-kilometers (18 miles) exclusion zone around Chernobyl. The foreign countries were not endangered either. Nevertheless, it was clearly pointed out that an increased rate of cancer patients could be expected in the disaster area in the long term.

According to official information, there are no Chernobyl residents among the 299 patients now hospitalized. According to the Soviet doctor, most of the victims were firefighters who knew where and against what they were being used.

As a consequence of this disaster, the Soviet Union will participate in an international medical database at Gale's suggestion. According to Gale, material on the experience gained in unprecedented cases of contamination will be jointly evaluated and published.

OPEN REACTIONS

Indirectly, the Soviet Union has now responded for the first time to the question of whether it will compensate neighboring countries, in particular Poland, in connection with the nuclear accident.

In the Kremlin's foreign policy magazine *Novoye Vremya* (The New Times), such an alleged reader inquiry is answered negatively. According to the magazine's justification, the emission of radioactivity was insignificant, short-lived and low.

Contrary to Polish measurements, the magazine claims that radioactivity in the countries bordering the Soviet Union increased only five times as much as normal. Therefore, Soviet goods and means of transport posed no danger, neither to the population nor to foreign countries.

In the meantime, the Soviet media continue their reporting on the course and victims of the accident. In almost all newspapers there are sometimes even half page reports and portraits of individual victims.

Eyewitnesses also report on the night of the accident itself, in which individual experts risked and lost their lives with their heroic efforts.

In this context, the party newspaper *Pravda* mentions a tenth fatality: a man who, fully aware of the danger, dived under radioactive water to lock a valve for the supply of hydrogen.

Komsomolskaya Pravda published the picture and story of a 23-year-old firefighter who, along with other named victims, faced fire and radioactivity during the night in question.

Individual workers and brigades donate part of their wages to the bereaved of the victims and to the evacuees. The newspapers regularly publish account numbers to which donations can be made.

Several artists have already announced charity concerts. Meanwhile, Party Leader Gorbachev confirmed at a meeting with the American doctor Robert Gale and the big industrialist Armand Hammer that he was ready for a meeting with President Reagan.

He thanked the two Americans for their commitment to the care of radiation victims. For the meeting with Reagan, Gorbachev demanded however an improved political atmosphere.

In his statement on Chernobyl, the Soviet party leader had already spoken of a campaign of rampant Anti-Sovietism in the USA. At the same time, on the other hand, he had offered the American president to meet with him immediately anywhere in the world to sign an agreement to stop nuclear testing.

Встреча М. С. Горбачева с А. Хаммером и Р. Гейлом

15 мая М. С. Горбачев принял в Кремле видного американского предпринимателя и общественного деятеля А. Хаммера и доктора Р. Гейла. Он выразил глубокую признательность за проявленное ими сочувствие, понимание и быструю конкретную помощь в связи с постигшей советских людей бедой — аварией на Чернобыльской АЭС. Их благородный поступок отразил чувства многих простых американцев и общественных деятелей, которые шлют сейчас в Москву искренние, трогательные письма и телеграммы. Некоторые из них М. С. Горбачев показал собеседникам.

В поступке А. Хаммера и Р. Гейла, подчеркнул М. С. Горбачев, советские люди видят пример того, как должны были бы строиться отношения между двумя великими народами при наличии политической мудрости и воли у руководства обеих стран.

Однако поведение официального Вашингтона в эти трудные дни вызывает глубокое разочарование: это постыдная спекуляция на несчастье, беспардонные попытки использовать случившееся, чтобы дискредитировать всю политику Советского Союза, посеять недоверие к его миролюбивым инициативам. Народы дадут свою оценку позиций каждого перед лицом этой трагедии и, надеемся, сделают правильные выводы, прежде всего о том, что необходимо удвоить, удесятерить усилия в борьбе против ядерных испытаний, за ликвидацию ядерного оружия и обеспечить надежное международное сотрудничество в использовании мирного атома.

М. С. Горбачев сообщил собеседникам, что ситуацию в районе аварии удалось взять под контроль, что люди там работают самоотверженно, героически. Задействован весь потенциал советской науки, чтобы эффективно ликвидировать последствия и извлечь все необходимые уроки.

Первейший долг сейчас — помочь людям, пострадавшим от аварии. Самое ценное — это человек, каждая жизнь. И главная забота Советского государства — сделать все возможное для охраны и восстановления здоровья людей, возместить понесенный ими ущерб.

М. С. Горбачев поинтересовался у доктора Гейла, как у него идут дела по лечению пострадавших. Р. Гейл рассказал, что уже сделано и что можно еще сделать. Он высоко отозвался о работе своих коллег — советских врачей. Подчеркнул, что все в мире должны теперь понять, что, если разразится ядерная война, никакая медицина уже ничего не сможет сделать, она будет просто никому не нужна.

В беседе, по инициативе А. Хаммера, был затронут вопрос о советско-американской встрече на высшем уровне. М. С. Горбачев подтвердил свое принципиальное согласие на новую встречу, повторив, что для ее проведения нужны две простые вещи: готовность к тому, чтобы она принесла ощутимый практический результат хотя бы в одном-двух вопросах, волнующих весь мир, и соответствующая политическая атмосфера.

Что касается первого, встреча не может произойти по американскому сценарию, чего, видимо, хотят от нас добиться. Так же, как ее не будет и по советскому сценарию. Надо искать общую платформу с ориентацией на конкретный результат. Что касается атмосферы, то она еще более ухудшилась в результате злостной антисоветской кампании, развернутой Вашингтоном по поводу аварии в Чернобыле.

В заключение теплой, откровенной беседы М. С. Горбачев еще раз поблагодарил А. Хаммера и доктора Гейла.

В беседе принял участие секретарь ЦК КПСС А. Ф. Добрынин.

(ТАСС)

Во время беседы.

Фото Ю. Лизунова и В. Великжанина (ТАСС).

Gorbachev meets Armand Hammer and Robert Gale.
Article in *Pravda*, May 17, 1986.

ARMAND HAMMER

The best friend of the Soviet Union in America is very old and very wealthy: Armand Hammer, a capitalist who has been loyal to the communist superpower for 65 years.

Hammer was still a young doctor when he first came to Russia in 1921. He wanted to help a country shaken by revolution and civil war – with medical supplies and an emergency hospital. His motive: Hammer's father was a Russian emigrant who had co-founded a communist labor movement in America. But Hammer's idealism was joined by a good portion of business acumen. He saw that food was needed more than medicine. Personal contacts with Lenin and the famine at that time brought Hammer large delivery orders. Hammer himself reports on his transformation from a doctor to a merchant. It was Lenin himself who told him: "We have enough doctors. What we need are business people".

Ennobled by this Lenin quotation, Hammer has remained one of the most important and reliable trading partners for the Soviet Union to this day, and one who knew how to successfully combine politics and business. With his good relations he brought many American companies to the Soviet market and opened the chapter of East-West trade.

When Hammer left the Soviet Union after a longer stay at the beginning of Stalin's reign, he brought home art treasures from the tsarist era worth several million dollars. He had bought them from the aristocracy, impoverished by the revolution. For his art treasures he founded a large gallery in New York. In addition, Hammer turned a small whisky brewery into a successful corporation.

In 1957 he took over an almost bankrupt oil company, which today is a leading company in the USA under the name Occidental Petroleum. When American President Kennedy needed a crisis mediator between Washington and Moscow, he sent Armand Hammer to the Kremlin in 1961. The negotiator did more than the White House instructed him to do:

In a personal conversation with Khrushchev, Hammer drew up a billion-dollar supply contract for fertilizer for the next twelve years. Another billion-dollar business was a gas pipeline that Hammer laid for the Soviets through Siberia to the Sea of Japan.

Party leader Brezhnev rewarded him with his own apartment in the Soviet metropolis. Hammer also set himself up a personal monument in Moscow, an international trade center with a luxury hotel, Japanese restaurant, Italian café and German beer bar. The only blemish: normal Russians can't get into it – only those with hard Western currency may enter. Hammer is the most popular American in the Soviet Union. He sends his art collections through the country and is allowed to jet behind in a private plane.

When he now referred the American bone marrow specialist Robert Gale to Moscow, the 88-year-old Hammer explained to the international press: All expenses for foreign aid, medicines, doctors and transport for the victims of Chernobyl were his personal gift to the Soviet people. The applauding Russians, who listened to him, had tears in their eyes.

THIRTY THOUSAND SQUARE METERS DISINFECTED

According to Soviet television, an area of 30,000 square meters has already been decontaminated around the Chernobyl reactor. The evening film report did not reveal how they fought the radioactivity. It also remained unclear to what extent buildings had already been included in this decontamination program. Those responsible obviously still see a danger for the adjoining bodies of water.

On the banks of the nearby Pripyat River, the camera showed sandy hills enriched with chemicals and protected by plastic tarp. This is to prevent radioactivity from entering the neighboring bodies of water. For the further "burial" of the reactor, as it is officially called, building brigades with cement mixing machines and trucks from many Soviet republics come to Chernobyl. After insulation work from above, a tunnel is now to be dug under the reactor, from which a kind of concrete sarcophagus protects the site of the accident in the ground.

The depiction was given over the weekend by Soviet Deputy Prime Minister Ivan Silayev. First, however, remote-controlled technology is to be used directly at the reactor site in order not to endanger further human lives. So far, an armored bulldozer has been used to try to recover contaminated debris from the explosion.

In a *Pravda* article about the news program *Vremya* on Soviet television, the meanwhile improved reporting on the reactor accident is indirectly praised. Literally the article goes on: "But the possibilities of reporting are not exhausted yet". In addition to Chernobyl, which has become a permanent topic for news and rumors alike, a new domestic focus has emerged in the Soviet Union in recent days.

A radical change has taken place in the cultural sphere. The Association of Filmmakers fired almost all important functionaries at its congress. Instead, a spokesman in the fight against censorship and bureaucracy, the director Elem Klimov, was elected to head the association; some of his films had not been allowed to be shown for a decade. The more than 600 delegates had fought against the so-called old guard in the film business in their own way: With loud clapping they prevented the film minister from continuing his speech. In the following sharp debates, the delegates spoke out against being patronized by the authorities and also demanded greater economic independence for the filmmakers.

A WAR
ON DIFFERENT FRONT LINES

The Soviet Union is in a war on different front lines. It is fighting against the consequences of the Chernobyl nuclear accident. It fights against emerging discontent and rumors among its own population. And finally, it is fighting against a bitter loss of prestige abroad as a result of a dishonest information policy.

Nothing is in order. On the contrary. The vehement, militant language of the media shows that the clashes continue in all areas.

Almost symbolically, soldiers in uniform adorn the front page of the army newspaper *Krasnaya Zvezda* (Red Star). They also fight against the invisible enemy, spraying their chemicals from armored cars against radioactive contamination. Anyone who lives in the Soviet Union as an observer, but is emotionally involved, will have gone through several phases:

– Anger at the widespread political dealings with the other affected countries immediately after the catastrophe.

– Fear about the gradually revealed extent of deaths and injuries. And finally:

– Compassion for the human problems of almost one hundred thousand evacuees.

Families have been torn apart and are still searching for each other. Despair reigns over the uncertain future, coupled with grief over the loss of homes and farms: For these people are gradually realizing that a return to the old settlement areas seems impossible for decades to come.

The paths of those affected are already separating. There are those who are already struggling with the courage of despair to build a new existence elsewhere in the Soviet Union. They can be transferred to distant parts of the country in order to have work and housing again. And then there are the many Ukrainians and Belarussians who have ties to their homeland and who cannot imagine continuing their old lives under completely new conditions.

They all have one depressing certainty in common:

For years to come, they will remain statistical examination material for doctors who have no comparable experience in dealing with such a catastrophe. None of the hundreds of thousands will escape the fate of belonging to a high-risk group, even without obvious radiation damage.

Whoever sees the evening television pictures of the old mothers with wrinkled faces and colorfully printed headscarves, whoever observes the children in the examination lines of the thousands of medical specialists, cannot help but feel a sorrowful solidarity with these people.

But the intolerance over the mistakes of the Soviet leadership, the anger over the failure of those responsible – all this probably prevails in the West.

The word "solidarity" is not a popular headline, but the "demand for compensation" is. It is difficult to measure what damage to the people and the economy has been done. But haggling in pennies over losses, the real extent of which cannot even be causally determined, seems a little greedy if not absurd. And here one can see the strange circle of those who find more words of self-justification than words of solidarity.

It was Genrich Borovik, the most media-effective television commentator of the Soviet Union, who turned the tables:

As a Soviet citizen, he demanded compensation for the moral damage the Soviet Union had suffered from the West.

His proof was in the headlines of western newspapers which – after the catastrophe became known – claimed in bold letters that tens of thousands of contaminated victims lied buried in a radioactive mass grave.

This sharp-tongued, cynical commentator did what he accused others of: confusing cause and effect.

Chernobyl is a challenge – not to the political superiority of a system, but to the sense of responsibility of all people. The demand for solidarity would go further on both sides than the outcry for compensation.

May 22, 1986

ADVICE
AGAINST RADIOACTIVITY

"Take a water glass, fill it with vodka, add the juice of a squeezed garlic clove and a dash of red wine. This mixture – drunk in one go – gives the body the necessary defenses against the threat of radioactive contamination."

Such nonsense is now circulating among Soviet citizens as a rumor or as an ironically meant recipe. A consequence of a lack of information about what radiation damage can do. The first tentative indications in the state press made it clear that regular lessons in radioactivity were appropriate, especially among the evacuated rural population in Ukraine and Belarus. But in the meantime – as the deputy health minister of the Soviet Union, Oleg Shchepin (1932-2019), criticized – even people in Moscow, Leningrad and Riga stormed the hospitals because they still felt – although hundreds of miles away from the scene of the accident – threatened by contradictory gossip.

With an enlightening interview published by *Literaturnaya Gazeta*, the health politician wants to clarify prevention and consequences. Vodka and red wine as medicines, according to the vice-minister, are in any case "fantasies of the purest kind". Quite the opposite, he criticizes this meanwhile common opinion with the reference: Taken straight with radioactivity, alcohol causes even more additional damage.

In order to prevent the greatest fears, a special center was established in the Soviet capital, where each traveler from the disaster area could have his clothes examined for radiation.

After all, the representative of the Ministry of Health admits that the approximately one hundred thousand residents who have been evacuated so far must be observed for years to come. The initial ease with which people were promised a speedy return to normal life in their old surroundings is no longer noticeable.

In the meantime, many Soviet citizens have cancelled their trips to the traditional holiday regions on the Black Sea, the Baltic Sea and to the Carpathians, because they fear the long-term consequences of the disaster there. Here, too, the official information is intended to reassure: "There is no doubt about the harmlessness of these areas."

Just as important as the purely medical consequences is the psychological pressure on those affected. In the state media it is reported proudly how the evacuees are helped with prudence and care. However, doctors are observing more and more psychological breakdowns.

The very fact that families had to leave their homes and farms overnight and children were separated from their parents, was described by Vice-Minister Shchepin in his very open conversation as an "enormous psychological burden". His conclusion at the end of the interview is astonishing. For the politician particularly criticizes the attitude of many scientists who had forgotten their own responsibility in the face of Chernobyl; they would not defend themselves against the many rumors with their knowledge.

To put it plainly: Even among the Soviet intelligentsia, there is sometimes more fear than enlightenment after the catastrophe.

ACADEMICIAN VELIKHOV
ABOUT THE CATASTROPHE

Yevgeny Velikhov, a leading nuclear scientist in the Chernobyl disaster operation, spoke soberly to the press:

"I don't want to give you the illusion," - he meant literally - "that all our questions have been solved".

The man, who had already informed the public that after the reactor accident a major catastrophe could only be prevented with great difficulty, explained that for days there had been fears that radioactivity would spread into the groundwater. According to Velikhov, even now the reactor can only be controlled from above and below. But what happens inside remains largely unclear.

Velikhov officially confirmed the number of 19 deaths that the reactor accident has caused so far. When asked how long the scientist expected the disaster area to be repopulated, Velikhov evaded the question: The first two of the four reactor units were to be put back into operation in just a few months and workers were to be deployed to do so. But he did not see a quick return of the population to this area.

In another context, Velikhov stressed that it was now a matter of isolating the radioactivity around the reactor for decades to come. This indicated that repopulation could take just as long.

The scientist had already caused a sensation because he had flown over the blown-up reactor more than forty times by helicopter at low altitude.

During his first television interview, which was subsequently broadcast from Chernobyl, he made a strained and exhausted impression. Now he confirmed that medical checks had not revealed any health risk to him. Speculations about this had become loud when the front page of *Pravda* wrote:

"The Ukrainian people will never forget the heroic dedication of this scientist".

Even after the first weeks of intensive work on the site, Velikhov was unable to name the exact cause of the accident. In addition to a few coincidences, he also suspected negligence on the part of the operating personnel. Because – so his argumentation – if they had behaved correctly, then such an accident would not have happened. At the same time, Velikhov pleaded for the further expansion of nuclear energy, even in the light of current experience.

Half ironically and half self-critically, he reduced the American concern about the reactor accident to the sentence: "When something like this happened in the USA, the Soviet scientists argued that their reactors were safer. Now it's the other way around. That is why we should now work for improved safety conditions for nuclear energy within an international framework."

FIRST INVESTIGATION REPORT

The official investigation report on the cause and extent of the Chernobyl disaster shocked the Soviet public.

What was discussed in the Moscow Politburo, the party's highest governing body, and published in extracts in Soviet newspapers, is enough to cast doubt on the functioning of the state apparatus. The ministries responsible have failed, and the public prosecutor's office is investigating a large number of high-ranking members of the government. Party reprimands and party exclusions are on the increase.

According to the Politburo report, a whole series of gross violations of the operating rules for nuclear power plants were to blame for the accident. It is said literally:

"It was found that the accident had been caused by a whole series of gross violations of the operating regulations of the reactor plants for which the employees of this plant were directly responsible."

"Irresponsibility" and "sloppiness" are the buzzwords of the criticism that the Soviet public is now facing. In addition to the official deaths of 28 people (an Israeli doctor who treated victims of the catastrophe in a Moscow hospital reported at least 30 deaths), the extent of the necessary mass investigations of "several hundred thousand affected people" was admitted for the first time. The contaminated area is believed to cover 620 square miles. The direct damage to property, harvest and production, without the resulting costs, is already estimated at approx. three billion US dollars.

The measures to contain the still existing danger are gigantic. In order to protect the groundwater around Chernobyl, a rainwater collection and drainage system needs to be put in place, which will continue to flush radioactivity from the air, trees and shrubs to the ground. The Pripyat River, near Chernobyl, is protected by a 20 kilometer (twelve miles) earth wall. Unofficially in Moscow it can be heard that the damaged reactor is to be encased by a hundred-meter-deep (approx. 330 feet) concrete wall in order to ward off dangers to the groundwater.

Meanwhile, the evacuated population is being prepared for the fact that a large number of them will not be able to return to their old homes. In the Republic of Belarus bordering Ukraine, the ministries have already ordered the first resettlement of evacuees, north of the danger zone. In the restricted area itself, more and more contaminated earth has to be removed.

According to the Politburo report, new safety regulations are to be developed for all nuclear power plants in the Soviet Union. In addition, the Communist Party wants to use an unusual measure to strengthen its control in the nuclear power plants by sending party supervisors, who are not subordinate to the plant management and the local party secretaries, but only to the Central Committee in Moscow.

Meanwhile, the newly appointed director of the Chernobyl nuclear power plant surprised the public with the news that the first and second reactor units (the fourth unit had had the accident) will be put back into operation in October of this year. The prerequisite for this is, however, that "still open" technical issues are resolved.

The special rhythm of work in Chernobyl shows, however, that the danger for the people there has by no means yet been averted. The experts are only allowed to stay for two weeks without interruption in the restricted area around the reactor and then spend a further two weeks in another place for a break and medical examination before they can return to their dangerous workplace.

Chernobyl also has psychologists who look after the workers at the scene of the accident. This seems to be necessary.

Pravda complained that more than 3,000 Chernobyl workers had found new jobs elsewhere. Another thousand skilled workers had been sent on vacation. The lack of manpower and ineffective measures of the local Communist Party leadership are considered by the party paper to be the most serious obstacles in the fight against the consequences of the disaster.

A ROCK STAR PRAYS FOR SALVATION[40]

Alla Pugacheva steps onto the stage in her golden tinsel robe, shakes her long curly red hair, spreads her arms and calls out to the audience of the Moscow Olympic Hall: "Money is money. But today we want to give our hearts, send our optimism to Chernobyl." What would sound like theatrical kitsch to other stars is convincing to the 35-year-old rock queen of the Soviet Union. With 150 million records sold as a popular amplifier, she did the impossible immediately: Within two weeks she had set up the first privately initiated rock concert for the victims of Chernobyl. She achieved a breakthrough in a country whose bureaucratic hurdles often enough drive even high party officials to despair.

Alla Pugacheva is spontaneous. As she told some journalists before the concert: "When I saw the first film reports from Chernobyl, it grabbed me! I just had to do something!"

Her way led directly to the Central Committee of the Communist Party, where she got permission and support. And by the way, she also managed to bring a new music group to the podium in front of the thirty thousand visitors, whose songs had so far only circulated as secret, pirate copies from the underground of the Moscow youth scene. The sympathy and solidarity with Chernobyl has proven to be stronger than the Soviet bureaucracy in recent weeks.

---

[40] Published in the German weekly newspaper *DIE ZEIT*, No. 24, 1986

Chernobyl also changed the Soviet citizens. With astonishing composure, they had initially accepted the abstract reports about the reactor accident. A lack of information about the dangers of radioactivity prevented panic. This was followed by a brief period of bitter, sarcastic humor, an answer to inaccurate information, based on the motto: "There is no such thing as radioactivity – and it is also constantly decreasing". When, however, the state mass media changed their information policy, no longer hid human suffering; when the number of fatalities rose and the "new heroes in the fight against the fourth reactor " were born and in many cases posthumously praised at the same time, the mood in the country changed.

The images of firefighters, mostly in their mid-twenties, with boyish features on their faces, marching directly into the radioactivity to prevent worse – they have done more than any political propaganda. They have awakened feelings, aroused compassion. These determined men have become positive heroes in a struggle that, for many Soviet citizens, has become even more lonely, but also more unequivocal, as a result of the reaction in some Western countries.

"How can you talk about compensation payments from the Soviet Union for the foreign countries affected by Chernobyl, when tens of thousands of our people have lost their belongings, hundreds are in hospitals and dozens are dying?" said a 30-year-old Soviet friend, more disappointed than reproached. "Do you not see that a tragedy of catastrophic proportions has hit especially our people first?"

Since Gorbachev took a stand on Chernobyl on television, this inward view has been reinforced even further. The tenor is that foreign countries do not want anything good for us – apart from simple people and individual personalities such as the American industrial magnate Armand Hammer.

When this great benefactor of the Soviet Union, who was still a friend of Lenin, told the press that the medical aid he had provided was his gift to the Soviet people, Russian journalists applauded with tears in their eyes. But the Soviet media usually reacted negatively to concerns beyond the borders.

The Kremlin's foreign policy in-house magazine in English, *The New Times*, played down a reader's question from England: The leakage of radioactivity was "short-lived, insignificant and minor". They also said that "falsehoods had been circulated that Soviet exports and means of transport were dangerous".

But the fight against rumors and "contradictory gossip" – according to *Literaturnaya Gazeta* – is also being waged within the Soviet Union. A deputy health minister tried to warn Soviet citizens that vodka and red wine are not panaceas against radioactivity. He criticized and revealed that hundreds of miles away from Chernobyl people in Moscow, Leningrad or Riga were coming to hospitals because they feared for their health. Even the attitude of many scientists leaves much to be desired, according to the health politician. For they had forgotten their own responsibility and had not used their knowledge to put up a fight against all the rumors.

To put it plainly: Even among the Soviet intelligentsia there was more fear than enlightenment in many places. The government newspaper *Izvestia* attempted to use a letter campaign to allay its readers' fears of the traditional holiday regions on the Black Sea, the Baltic Sea and in the Carpathians, which are considered "contaminated" by the population. Many Soviet citizens therefore gladly returned their "putyovka", their travel confirmation for one of the holiday regions, in order to make room for the evacuees from Ukraine.

For despite the use of science and technology, despite remote-controlled bulldozers that clean up the most heavily contaminated zone and despite heroic helicopter pilots who – according to the trade union newspaper *Trud* – are "trained in the war of Afghanistan": precise data on the nature and extent of the rays emitted are still lacking.

If the Chernobyl guards appear without a mask in front of the Soviet television reporter's camera, but at the same time the army newspaper *Krasnaya Zvezda* shows masked figures decontaminating the soil in the nuclear power area, then contradictions remain for the Soviet citizen: How bad is it really?

The contaminated area 18 miles around Chernobyl is now being called "The Zone". If all cattle had to be evacuated from this "zone", but are now grazed and milked peacefully with uncontaminated cows – what about the milk, what about the meat?

The precautionary measures in Ukraine and Belarus are strict: in some areas only pasta and rice are being delivered. Even if television shows a flourishing agriculture and gives the impression that the new Chernobyl "zone" border is ing the radiation from escaping, fears and doubts are now being voiced. Unofficial protest groups are turning against the so called "peaceful atom". They're collecting signatures for petitions to have the Soviet nuclear energy program reviewed. The police recently reacted ambiguously: First they detained members of just such a group in Moscow's Gorky Park, but then they released the participants and even returned the signature list for the petition to the protesters.

The old lady, who pays five rubles into the donations account number 904 at the counter of the savings bank, doesn't have politics in mind. She is neither for nor against nuclear energy. Only one thing is important to her: "Since the Great Patriotic War[41] there has never been such a catastrophe for the people of our country. And you have to stick together like you did then."

Mikhail Ulyanov also wants to demonstrate this cohesion. He is an exemplary Soviet actor, especially for war films. According to his own admission, rock music is not his thing.

---

[41] World War II.

But Ulyanov did come to Alla Pugacheva's benefit concert, encountered modern electronic sounds for the first time in his life and then confessed in front of the audience:

"This music is an outcry, even a prayer for salvation from such catastrophes."

Chernobyl set the Soviet people in motion – in Alla's rock concert as well as at work, on the street, in school. But Chernobyl also raised doubts about the Soviet slogan of "safe progress".

"The 20th century has lost its mind," a rock singer chants repeatedly to the applause of the audience.

A statement that at least included the Soviet Union as well.

THE FIGHT WILL CONTINUE

"The battle with the radioactive poison is not over. It will continue."

With this statement today the party newspaper *Pravda* starts a report about the disaster site in Chernobyl. In the same article the leading nuclear scientist of the Soviet Union Yevgeny Velikhov admits that the offensive in the fight against the catastrophe will not only be carried out around the reactor but also under it, in the ground.

This latest and very detailed article feeds two fears:

First, the reactor itself still seems to be burning. And second, the nuclear scientist's comment no longer excludes the possibility that the radioactive melting process has penetrated the earth.

The oppressive scale of the catastrophe is now also becoming clear to Soviet citizens, especially as *Pravda* continues to quote the scientist literally:

"No one has yet come into contact with a similar disaster. The unusual situation demands decisions on problems that scientists and specialists have never had to deal with before."

Thousands of people from all parts of the Soviet Union are said to have been deployed at the scene of the accident. For the first time, the party paper admits that there were fears about the drinking water supply. Admittedly, the water samples should now be within the scope of the standard.

While Soviet television in particular wants to prove with reports from the affected area in Ukraine that there is no panic among the population, the news agency TASS surprised in a contribution from Kiev with some clear statements:

"All companies are working. But of course there is fear. Especially the parents worry about their children."

With the euphemistic reference to upcoming summer holidays, the TASS correspondent describes long lines of people at ticket counters for trains and planes. According to this official Soviet description, dozens of extra trains and special flight connections are to be used to bring the children affected from the evacuated areas to holiday camps. Meanwhile, eyewitnesses from the Kiev railway station in Moscow report that several special trains from Ukraine have already arrived. Correspondents who wanted to get an up-to-date picture of the situation of the travelers from Kiev were expelled from the station building by the police.

RESPONSIBLE PERSONS NAMED

Chernobyl and its catastrophic consequences can now no longer be debited to the account of a tragic industrial accident, even for Soviet citizens, since those responsible were publicly named. With the dismissal of the plant director and the chief engineer from the Chernobyl nuclear power plant, the first signals have been given. Experts who should have known how to limit the damage have failed. Previously, in a sudden decision such party members had been excluded from the ranks of the Communist Party, who had initially thought of themselves and not of others during the catastrophe.

But the criticism of those responsible, who took off when they were called upon to take action, cannot, of course, alleviate the bitterness of some evacuees, who are now complaining about their treatment with open letters of protest:

Bureaucratic obstacles, rejection and a lack of helpfulness are denounced and even brought to public attention by the party newspaper *Pravda.*

One can only be astonished to note that the consequences of the catastrophe are to a large extent heaped on the shoulders of the victims.

In the meantime, it has also become clear which problems must be overcome not only with the evacuees, but also with the contaminated areas: The crowds can no longer be moved from village to village at will. Now the government newspaper *Izvestia* has also had to admit that people have been left behind even in contaminated areas. To protect them, disinfection teams are now trying to wash away the radioactivity house by house and street by street.

But it remains unclear where the radioactive waste is going. The scraped-off soil level of several inches thickness from the disaster area must also be stored safely. But according to the Soviet press, exactly where this will happen still triggers guesswork. What is astonishing, however, is the openness with which the problems are being put on the table right now – shortly before the meeting of the Supreme Soviet, the Parliament. It cannot therefore be ruled out that the Members of Parliament at their regular meeting – which takes place only every six months – will now use the disaster of Chernobyl to demand further personnel consequences at party and government levels.

June 20, 1986

GORBACHEV'S RECKONING[42]

Mikhail Gorbachev has openly thrown down the gauntlet to his opponents in the party bureaucracy. But the Secretary General is reluctant to talk about Chernobyl.

At the plenary session of the Central Committee of Soviet Communists, Gorbachev returned to a verbal acuity that had seemed lost since the Party Conference at the beginning of the year. The reason for his anger: the efforts to convert the Soviet economy from quantity to quality and intensive use of modern technology are still encountering resistance throughout the country. This is shown by hair-raising examples that Gorbachev presented to his comrades as a deterrent.

The head of an electro-technical company, for example, had quickly reorganized the company and made a profit without the approval of a ministry and against the vote of the local party organization. Although the project was successful, his opponents instructed a prosecutor to investigate the head of the company. Although the investigations gave no cause for accusation, the dedicated company manager was excluded from the Communist Party.

According to Gorbachev, a letter in the manager's defense, written by benevolent colleagues, was intercepted by the local authorities, i.e. the KGB, at the post office and never reached Moscow. Initiative, demanded by the new rulers, is suspicious not only to the bureaucrats, but also to the Secret Service.

Gorbachev addressed the plenary with a warning undertone to those "who are trying to stop us". He threatened

---

[42]Published in the German weekly newspaper *DIE ZEIT*, No. 26, 1986.

the Party, that he would "prevent all efforts to copy old methods and mistakes". However, Gorbachev is not only fighting against the "blind belief in the omnipotence of the apparatus". He is also fighting against outdated machinery in the factories, against 20 percent crop loss due to lack of transport and storage conditions, against the useless burning of 13 billion cubic meters of natural gas annually. And he is also fighting against increases in production, which turned out to be economic damage.

Growth rates in mechanical engineering, for example, were always measured by weight. So those who used materials that were as heavy as possible had the best results, no matter how efficient a machine really was. Such nonsense is to be stopped with the coming Five-Year-Plan, which has now been forwarded to the Supreme Soviet, the Parliament, for approval. But Gorbachev's quote from Lenin – "illusions and self-deception are terrible, the fear of the truth is devastating" – as a guideline for this plenum did not persuade the Secretary General himself to also subject the Chernobyl catastrophe to critical discussion.

Out of three pages of newspapers that Gorbachev filled with his speech, only a sparse ten lines are dedicated to the greatest nuclear accident in human history. Here, too, he finds only words of condolence for the families affected and words of recognition for the whole country, which has stood up during this "hard test" to eliminate the consequences.

In the meantime, the Soviet citizens were able to find out from the Moscow press what kind of "consequences" these were. Since then, the disaster can no longer be debited to the account of a tragic industrial accident. With the dismissal of the Chernobyl plant director and chief engineer, specialists were found who should have known how to limit the damage. Members of the Communist Party had previously been expelled because, as the saying goes, they had only thought of themselves and not of the others when they were in need.

The criticism of those responsible, who failed or ran away when they were called upon to intervene, cannot dampen the bitterness of some evacuees who are now complaining about their treatment with open letters of protest. Bureaucratic obstacles, rejection and a lack of willingness to help are now being denounced and even being made public by the party newspaper *Pravda*. Meanwhile, it is also clear which new problems are emerging: The people from the contaminated areas cannot be evacuated as necessary. In Belarus, there was no shelter for the 7,000 inhabitants of Bragin, a district of the Gomel region, bordering directly on Chernobyl.

Although according to the newspaper *Izvestia* no one could live in Bragin, unscathed for months or even years. The inhabitants had been left behind and now have to content themselves with the fact that the decontamination is taking place in their presence – house by house, street by street. But where the radioactive material is to go remains unclear. These extremely critical reports appeared right at the meeting of the Supreme Soviet.

MYTHS AND REALITY

Chernobyl continues to fill the newspaper columns of the Soviet press. *Komsomolskaya Pravda* dedicated a whole special page to the "myths and reality of radioactive radiation" – as the headline says.

Above all, it was about curbing rumors concerning the continuing dangers. Meanwhile, government authorities in Belarus have decreed that part of the evacuated population may not return to their old homeland, but will be settled in new places. Although the radioactivity was only minor, the reason given was that the returning children, in particular, were not to be exposed to even the slightest amount of radiation.

In this situation, the newly appointed director of the Chernobyl nuclear power plant surprised in a conversation with the correspondent of the party newspaper *Pravda* with the news that the first and second reactor units are to be put back into operation as early as October.

The prerequisite for this restrictive remark was, however, that technical issues that were still open be resolved and, above all, that new safety regulations be passed by the responsible state investigation commission.

The third reactor , which was endangered by an overarching fire, will be left "frozen". The fourth reactor , into which a measuring probe for heat development has recently been driven, has already been buried under a mountain of five thousand tons of sand, lead and boron.

The special rhythm of the work at Chernobyl shows that the danger for the people there has by no means been averted. The experts are only allowed to stay in the restricted area for

14 days without interruption and are then taken away for a further two weeks for recreation and medical examination before they can return to their dangerous workplace. In addition, psychologists have been appointed to look after the workers on site in Chernobyl.

The same applies to many evacuated families, who are still struggling to adapt to their new situation.

In Chernobyl itself, other problems are emerging. For example, the new director of the nuclear power plant complained that more than three thousand workers had left the city and were looking for another job. Another thousand are on leave. The shortage of labor and ineffective measures by the local party leadership are therefore seen as the most serious obstacles to overcoming the consequences of the disaster.

NOT MUCH CRITICISM
FROM YOUNG PEOPLE

Moscow in the early evening. In Gorky Park city residents enjoy their free hours after work. From the loudspeakers at the massive entrance gate, Soviet hits are booming away. Just a few meters further on, a few young people have gathered. They are discussing together and waving papers in their hands towards the passers-by. They want to collect signatures to review the nuclear energy program in the Soviet Union. But their spontaneous protest meets with displeasure from the police. Some militiamen are quickly at hand; the opponents of nuclear power were led away. Only later does it become known that they were interrogated and then released. Even the list with only a few signatures was not confiscated. What outraged the militia was more the disruption of public order.

Opponents of nuclear power are hardly taken seriously in the Soviet Union. The declared goal of the national economy is the rapid expansion of nuclear energy. Even after Chernobyl, politicians and the mass media did everything they could to propagate this – in their opinion the cheapest and cleanest – source of energy. Nobody seems to be plagued by self-doubt, although for many years to come hundreds of thousands of Soviet citizens will have to deal with the consequences of the Chernobyl accident.

The few protest groups among young people who call themselves opponents of nuclear power have no public impact. Anyone who meets young people on the street or in the Komsomol Club, at work or at university to discuss the problem of nuclear power will usually be disappointed. Quite simply because, even after Chernobyl, too little is known about this energy. The most common reaction is to shrug one's shoulders, with the following argument: "Well, the accident at Chernobyl is bad, but after all it's not nuclear energy that's to blame but the sloppiness of the people themselves."

An average Soviet young person can hardly imagine what possible alternatives might look like that are often discussed in the West. Basically, all we know is that this huge country has always suffered from a lack of energy – and if people really want to do better, then they will undoubtedly accept nuclear power. However, there are already some doubts among experts as to how quickly nuclear energy should really be expanded. Rumors are also being spread that another nuclear power plant has allegedly been decommissioned because of sloppy maintenance – in the north of the Soviet Union, in the Baltic States. But the official propaganda of the government can keep pace with the advertising of the German nuclear industry. Glossy brochures and film reports praise progress with nuclear energy.

However, the Soviet youth's restraint in this matter is nothing special. For in many other areas, too, there is no such committed debate as in the West. Young people are educated to accept everything the state and the party have in mind. And instead of protesting against it, many seek the path of least resistance: They go out, take drugs, drink alcohol and let things slide at work. Some bribe their superiors with their meager monthly salaries so that they don't have to come to work at all. Instead, they trade on the black market. Soviet society has to struggle more with such phenomena among young people than with critical discussions about nuclear energy.

READERS' DISCUSSION
ON NUCLEAR ENERGY

A reader of *Pravda*, Comrade Dachno from Kiev, made a historical comparison. In view of the continuing uproar about Chernobyl in the Soviet Union, he recalls the invention of the railroad. "Back then" – Dachno philosophizes in a letter to the party newspaper – "the railroad was held responsible for many accidents. But technical progress cannot be stopped."

Comrade Dachno is an exception; because most of the letters to *Pravda* are worried inquiries about the future of nuclear energy.

Comrade Nechipurenko from Krasnodar suggests without further ado: "Put the nuclear power plants in deserted areas, in the tundra or in the desert".

A high-ranking politician, Andranik Petrosyants, who is responsible for the use of nuclear energy at the ministerial level, explains why such a request contradicts the interests of the Soviet economy.

Petrosyants also describes in detail the current situation of the fourth reactor : A cooled concrete slab has been installed under the accident reactor; further elements for heat exchange are located underneath; two hundred special thermometers have been installed underground one floor below to monitor possible heat developments.

Although a concerned reader still sees a source of danger in the fourth reactor because radioactivity is buried in what is now officially called the sarcophagus, Petrosyants believes that control over the reactor is assured for several decades.

The first and second reactor s are to be put back into operation – literally – "at the end of autumn this year".

Petrosyants does not want to fix an exact date, after the new director of Chernobyl had already set October 1ˢᵗ as the deadline.

No decision has yet been made on the third reactor . The situation there is complicated and only after extensive investigations will it be decided whether a repair is worthwhile or whether the third reactor must also be "buried", like the fourth block is already.

But the most important lesson learned by the state media from Chernobyl concerns the workers at the power plant themselves – because not nuclear energy, but the operating personnel failed: That is the tenor of the investigation report about the accident as well as the tenor of the answers to the readers.

What's more, the shortcomings in the construction of the Soviet nuclear power plants are no longer being concealed. Faulty material and negligent assembly contribute to the fact that - as several letters to the editor have shown - a number of new nuclear power plants are also in an unsatisfactory condition.

The *Pravda* editors responsible for this campaign do not reveal where the readers got this detailed information from.

However, the conclusion is clear: not only must the Soviet citizen work better and more precisely, but also the government is to blame for this Chernobyl disaster.

TV DOCUMENTARY RAISES HIGH EXPECTATIONS

With the spectacular announcement of a documentary film about Chernobyl, Soviet television had raised high expectations. Surprisingly, a popular music program was removed from the TV schedule in order to make way for the film about the catastrophe.

Heavy criticism in the press of the inadequate clean-up work, the sudden visit of the Soviet head of government Nikolai Ryzhkov (*1929) to the scene of the accident – all this gave the documentary film an unusual topicality.

But those who expected sensations were disappointed. Most of the pictures were already familiar to viewers from previous television news programs. In a chronology of events, the shortcomings of the initially sluggish reporting were concealed; instead, the film paid tribute to the first victims of Chernobyl in an impressive dramaturgy:

In a hurry, the camera chases once more through the empty corridors of the damaged fourth reactor . In this deserted scene, the viewer suddenly hears the hasty steps of a task force. Photos appear out of nowhere, floating in the foreground of the screen and disappearing just as suddenly: young faces with boyish features – firefighters sent to their deaths to save others.

These photos were first published on the pages of the government newspaper *Izvestia* and symbolize for Soviet citizens the lost battle against a technology that could not be mastered.

But the television film was not intended to remind the viewers so much of the defeat. The main motive was rather to try to show how the consequences of the misfortune had been mastered so far. In addition to the almost lyrical cruelty of delicate guitar music, to which military trucks are scanned with Geiger counters for their radiation in Chernobyl at night, the film shows the determined courage of hard-working miners and discussing scientists. The commentator's language was a true borrowing from war reporting. Example: "We are in a new stage. It's now moving from defense to attack." Although the images had long been familiar, this time too they left the oppressive impression of a battlefield:

Tanks with spraying attachments direct their decontaminating jet against small peasant cottages. Masked figures drill into the ground to encase the fourth reactor with cement. Unmanned bulldozers act as robots cleaning up the center of the catastrophe. In between, faded in, again and again the stationary carousel from an evacuated children's playground. A symbolic hint that the next generation must be protected from further harm. But the really frightening pictures from hospitals where radiation victims are treated were missing completely.

Instead, the camera captured the natural radiant power of the sun, which surrounds new settlements for the evacuees in the picturesque sunset.

However, Chernobyl is still a catastrophe. The film did not conceal this. But even from this disaster one can learn something – so the moral of the commentator. Namely how right the decision of the Soviet government was to stand up for a stop to the nuclear arms race.

AMBIGUITIES REMAIN

The situation at the Chernobyl accident site is still not quite clear to those responsible. Conflicting statements in the Soviet press and from politicians result in contradictory data. The government newspaper *Izvestia* wrote that the source of the fire had not yet been completely extinguished, thus confirming a statement by *Pravda* in which it literally said: "The battle with the radioactive poison has not yet ended." In contrast, responsible politicians in Kiev told correspondents that the "process of the fire had ended".

A desperate situation hides behind this: So far, the damaged reactor itself can only be observed from the air. The head of the Vienna Atomic Energy Agency, Hans Blix, also visited the scene of the accident with a helicopter and said on Soviet television that he had seen smoke rising.

Experts are still trying to bury the reactor under a mountain of sandbags, enriched with special chemical material, dropped from helicopters. Moreover, the leading Soviet nuclear scientist Evgeny Velikhov announced that the offensive in the fight against the catastrophe would not only be carried out around the reactor, but also under it – i.e. in the ground. This statement feeds the fear that the radioactive melting process has penetrated the soil. Unofficially, in Moscow it is at least made clear that the radioactive process has been contained but has not yet been stopped. The statement of the nuclear scientist Velikhov: "Nobody has yet come into contact with a similar accident. The unusual situation demands decisions on problems that neither scientists nor specialists have ever had anything to do with."

Meanwhile, Soviet television is continuing its appeasement campaign with reports from Ukraine. For the first time, an evacuated woman, who had been resettled on the collective farm "New Life", had her say. Without looking into the camera, she confirmed to the reporter that all necessary help had been given to her.

In the meantime, the Politburo of the Communist Party, has issued a decree on the disaster. It states that all those affected are entitled to the necessary damages and wage compensation. In addition, special benefits are granted to the numerous helpers in combating the disaster.

In a TASS declaration, however, the Soviet Union opposed import restrictions imposed by the European Community (EC). Such measures would contradict the international approach to trade. In addition, TASS assured that the Soviet Union would strictly check for radioactivity in foodstuffs as well as transport equipment in order to protect its own population and that of other countries.

As a sign of this activity, the television camera followed the use of such radiation measuring devices, which are now allegedly used on Ukrainian country roads and fields.

October 17, 1986

THE CONSEQUENCES OF CHERNOBYL[43]

In a report first published by the Politburo, the direct damage caused by Chernobyl was estimated at two billion rubles, the equivalent of about three billion US dollars. To date, this sum has not been broken down into specific damages; but in the meantime, many publications in the Soviet press have listed itemized costs of the damage losses in more detail.

THE PEOPLE:

According to official figures, 250 million rubles have so far been paid in financial compensation for the homes and possessions of those people who had been evacuated from the 30 km (18 miles) safety zone around the nuclear power plant. The families received on average 12 to 15-thousand rubles paid according to the following scale:

Four thousand rubles for a one-person household; seven thousand rubles for a two-person household; and 1,500 rubles for each additional family member.

However, as the latest evacuations have affected almost 130,000 people and the security zone has been extended on various occasions, the total amount of burden sharing will ultimately be even higher. For those evacuees who cannot return to their home villages, new shelters have been and are

---

[43] German weekly newspaper *DIE ZEIT*, No. 43, 1986. Material for the dossier *Tschernobyl: Ein Fehler nach dem anderen. (Chernobyl: One Mistake after the Other).*

being built. In the meantime, 53 new settlements with a total of 8,000 houses are said to have been completed.

According to the head of the regional government of Kiev, Ivan Plyushch (1941-2014), the compensations paid so far include – in addition to the compensations mentioned above – other payments made by the trade unions and the Red Cross, which are not yet registered.

The follow-up costs also include the construction of a new city for 30,000 people to house the skilled workers and families of the Chernobyl nuclear power plant. This site is located about 30 to 40 minutes by train northeast of Chernobyl and is expected to be ready for occupancy in two years.

In a very short time, the infrastructure of old villages in the southern tip of the apparently severely affected Republic of Belarus has been allegedly improved so that evacuees can also settle here. An area party secretary of Gomel announced that for this purpose over 160 miles of country roads were asphalted or newly constructed; in addition, almost one hundred wells had to be newly drilled and more than 1500 wells restored. Also, the network of water pipes was extended by 155 miles to supply the new settlers. These figures, however, only relate to part of the infrastructural services that have already been provided. In both affected areas of Kiev (Ukraine) and Gomel (Belarus), 320 million rubles have already been spent on such measures.

Two other important items are social welfare and medical care. In the meantime, more than 60,000 children have been sent free of charge to holiday areas. Moreover, many evacuees also spent the summer months free of charge in the spas and holiday homes on the Black Sea. Since the trade union traditionally provides considerable services for this, the expenses for these accommodations have not yet been billed through state agencies. According to the state commission, several hundred thousand people have been examined for radiation damage and possible consequences in the danger area. This measure required considerable capacity to be withdrawn from the normal medical service. More than ten thousand doctors and nursing staff are said to have been on duty. In addition, eyewitnesses still report considerable unrest among the population.

The hospitals in the affected area are still being confronted with a large number of patients, who at least take precautionary measures to seek treatment. In contrast – according to the Soviet press – out of 300 officially registered radiation patients, only two people remain in a special clinic in Moscow. Cosmetic operations are intended to compensate for their skin damage. A further 15 to 20 victims are only in hospital from time to time. All other survivors are already in rehabilitation centers. According to official figures, the number of deaths of a total of 31 – including six firefighters and the rest being nuclear power plant employees – has not increased so far. Among the population of the affected and contaminated areas, it has been repeatedly stated that "there are no life-threatening injuries at all as a result of Chernobyl".

THE REACTOR:

According to Soviet calculations, the loss of the fourth reactor will cost 400 million rubles for planning and construction. A further, still unknown sum must be estimated for the "burial" of the reactor. The Soviet Union also had to raise considerable foreign currency for this, because it bought concrete-spraying machines and remote-controlled cleaning machines from Western countries for cash payment. Also in the West, the Soviet Union had an expert report prepared on technical problems in setting the reactor in concrete. Any heat and radiation developments should be calculated in advance using computer simulations and secured accordingly. Unofficially it can be learned in Moscow that the costs for this expertise were "considerable".

Of the two companies that were active in an advisory capacity, one company already had experience with the Harrisburg reactor accident.

As a result of this expertise, the construction of an elaborate venting system with special filters was started, which is intended to defuse the reactor, embedded in concrete. Previously, a concrete slab had already been cast under the reactor, which could also dissipate any heat generated by a cooling system. For this purpose, a tunnel 136 meters long (almost 150 yards) had to be dug from the safer outer district to under the site of the accident. As reported, a total of 250,000 tons of concrete and thousands of tons of rolled metallic material were used to bury the entire complex in a concrete sarcophagus.

At the beginning of October 1986, it was announced in the press that the construction of a 52-meter deep retaining wall weighing almost 900 tons would begin. This underground wall will shield the fourth reactor and will then be covered with earth and plants.

Also at the beginning of October, the date for the re-start of the first two undamaged reactors was announced. However, after a short power test, the operation of the first reactor had to be stopped again because – as it was generally said – false signals had appeared. Two days spent searching for the defect were interpreted by the Soviet press as "great care now being taken in the operation of the nuclear power plant". Since then the trial operation has continued, as the new plant director Erik Nikolaevich Pozdyshev (*1937) confirmed in an interview with the party newspaper *Pravda* on October 10, 1986.

At the same time, he announced that the second and the damaged third would also be connected to the grid. In addition, the construction of the fifth and sixth , which was interrupted by the accident, will be resumed. In this connection, *Pravda* speaks of a skeptical attitude against the further construction of new reactors, which the new nuclear power plant director, however, rejects with reference to the necessity of nuclear energy.

THE ECONOMY:

So far, reliable statements about the consequences and losses for the economy are hardly possible. Data on crop failures among Western experts in Moscow vary between a few hundred thousand and a few million tons of grain. Calculations based on the contaminated areas – officially 620 square miles had been described as contaminated – must take into account the fact that the less agriculturally used swamp zone northwest of Chernobyl is affected. For exports, this question plays almost no role at all, because only two percent of total Soviet exports to the West are agricultural products.

What remains unclear is what happened to the livestock evacuated from the contaminated area and housed on other collective farms. Although regular radiation measurements at the food companies and the markets have been made mandatory by the state, nothing reliable is known about the whereabouts of radiated meat and dairy products. Only once had the official authorities said that fresh milk was processed into cheese and butter to break down substances with short half-lives during storage.

Quite serious is the Chernobyl energy blackout. The power plant last produced 29 billion kilowatts in full operation in 1985. This means that the Ukrainian economy, in particular, has lost twelve billion kilowatt hours since the accident. The astonishing decision to switch the nuclear power plant on again now can be explained by energy bottlenecks that occur in the Soviet Union, especially during the winter months. Moreover, since other power plants – as recently criticized by *Pravda* in an editorial – do not produce their full output either, the loss of Chernobyl also has an overall negative impact on the economy.

Despite the relatively open and vivid reports, Chernobyl still raises a number of questions:

- What is the real level of soil contamination in the 30-kilometer (18 miles) zone? According to a statement made to the Atomic Energy Agency in Vienna, only air measurements that are regularly taken along the western border of the Soviet Union and at a site 38 miles from Chernobyl are communicated abroad.
- Who will compensate for the withdrawal of hundreds of millions of tons of building materials from the already battered construction industry to eliminate the consequences of the disaster?
- From which budgets (federal, regional, local) do the funds for compensation and new acquisitions come? This will also have a major impact on the regional economic structure of the affected areas.

Finally, there are still unforeseeable social problems to overcome. Evacuees now report looting of their abandoned homes. Newspapers complain that those returning still spread many rumors among the population that lead to insecurity. It is claimed that the nuclear power plant is still leaking radioactivity. In addition, the extent of the flight-like population movement and the loss of workers have barely been mentioned by the Soviet press.

December 9, 1986

HEROIC BATTLE ON THE SCREEN

The heroic battle surrounding the fourth reactor of Chernobyl was followed by millions of Soviet citizens on TV. A concrete sarcophagus was created, so to speak, with the cameras looking on, literally burying the scene of the accident. Helicopters threw bags, filled with sand and lead, onto the shattered reactor. The floor of the tunnel below the reactor was covered with massive amounts of poured concrete. Remote-controlled, robotic bulldozers pushed the radioactive discharge of the explosion together. But since recently, Soviet citizens have known that they could not see the whole truth on the screen.

Even the remote-controlled robots themselves allegedly failed due to excessive radiation exposure. Therefore, as Major General Nikolai Tarakanov (*1934) meticulously described in the military newspaper *Krasnaya Zvezda*, the radioactive waste had to be disposed by human hands. The task was complicated and dangerous: At a height of 70 to 140 meters (approx. 75 to 150 yd.) on the edges of the burst reactor building, ejected lumps of graphite and fuel elements kept the fourth from being closed up with a concrete roof structure. Volunteers were hoisted up by helicopter in 20 kilograms (44 lb.) of heavy protective clothing to throw the remnants of the explosion down into the reactor's "throat" with spades and pickaxes. Preliminary measurements showed that such a shift could not last longer than a minute in the most dangerous places. The army newspaper mentions a radiation intensity of 3.6 roentgen, which affected the volunteers.[44]

---

[44] In 1950, the International Commission on Radiation Units and Measurements (ICRP) reduced their recommended limit to 0.3 roentgen

This special mission, which had previously been kept secret, lasted from September 17 to October 1, i.e. about two weeks. According to the newspaper, the decision to do it manually was not an easy one. After a long debate, the government commission itself decided on this procedure, because otherwise the reactor could not have been completely sealed.

The largest chunk of material that had to be handled weighed 350 kilograms (770 lb.). It was encircled by lead bands with which the helpers had to move the contaminated colossus out of the way within forty seconds. After the successful completion of this operation, the special troop celebrated this victory by hoisting the red flag of the Soviet Union on the reactor's ventilation pipe. The article in the army newspaper does not mention whether the volunteers have been affected by the health consequences of this operation in the immediate danger zone. It also remains unclear which ground radiation has been measured by the Soviet side since the Chernobyl accident.

There are still strict precautionary measures around Chernobyl. Nevertheless, Western skilled workers employed at foreign companies in the region about 155 miles from Chernobyl recently complained that contaminated bread had appeared. It has also become known that radiation measuring equipment belonging to Western representatives at these firms, have disappeared or been damaged. Despite a relatively open treatment of the nuclear accident, a discussion of the consequences of Chernobyl is still considered taboo in some cases.

---

per week for whole-body exposure. Retrieved May 29, 2020 under https://en.wikipedia.org/wiki/Roentgen_(unit)

ANNUAL REVIEW

The Chernobyl disaster did not raise any doubts in official Soviet politics about the accelerated expansion of nuclear energy.

On the contrary, it was not until this year that the Soviet Union, together with the other Comecon countries, adopted an energy program based mainly on nuclear power stations.

The Soviet representative to the UN Commission on Energy and the Environment, which was currently meeting in Moscow, was also not being plagued by any doubts in view of the ongoing Chernobyl discussion in this forum.

With so much enthusiasm for nuclear energy, the question is what consequences at all the Soviet Union has drawn from the lessons of Chernobyl.

First and foremost, there is the concern to ensure the health of those who live in the immediate Chernobyl catchment area. The measures taken are gigantic: Several hundred thousand people have been medically examined; thousands of square meters of soil have now been removed; countless bushes, hedges and trees, which could be carriers of radioactive fallout, have been cut down to the roots. Entire villages and small towns have so far been decontaminated, sometimes by laborious manual labor. All this can be proven not only by Soviet reporting, but also by witness statements.

However, the situation in the food sector is unclear: The first complaints from Western skilled workers in the affected region were raised when, allegedly, radioactive-contaminated bread was put on the table. It is therefore to be feared that perhaps not the entire harvest affected was destroyed, but was processed after a certain waiting period. Such action had already been announced for dairy products. Fresh milk was not to be delivered, but processed into butter and cheese so that "the radioactive substances could decompose over time".

At the scene of the accident itself, the exploded fourth reactor was buried – sometimes under dramatic circumstances – in a concrete sarcophagus.

Unit one and two, on the other hand, have been put back into operation. It is still being investigated to what extent the consequences of the fires in the third reactor make it possible to put it back into operation. In addition, the nuclear power plant will be expanded further, because Chernobyl had not been completely built at the time of the disaster.

In the meantime, experts are said to have inspected all similar reactors in the Soviet Union in order to rule out possible sources of danger for the future. Chernobyl plant managers in charge and political officials have already had to vacate their seats. They have been accused of unbelievable carelessness, which was largely to blame for the disaster.

However, other nuclear power stations within the Soviet Union also appear to be subject to stricter controls. In Armenia, for example, a nuclear power plant has not been in operation for some time after an incident occurred there. Other power plants are reported not to have supplied the desired amount of electricity – for whatever reasons, that remains unclear.

At present, only the Soviet advertising for the export of nuclear power plants seems to have been curbed. When party leader Gorbachev recently visited India, a country that receives massive energy policy support from the Soviet Union, not a word was said about nuclear energy. Instead, the Soviet Union gave a billion-dollar loan to modernize conventional power stations.

THE YEAR 1987

February 19, 1987

"WARNING"
NEW DOCUMENTARY FILM
ABOUT CHERNOBYL

Under the title "Warning", Soviet television has already broadcast its second documentary film about the events at Chernobyl. This time it was about harsh criticism of the local authorities, who had reacted helplessly. The Ukrainian health minister was accused of having waited nine days before informing the population about security measures.

After all, there had been a lack of first aid, not even bandages for the victims.

Despite this harsh criticism, however, there is no worried undertone about the use of nuclear energy. Quite the opposite – as if it were a holiday, the moment was captured by the camera when the first reactor after the accident went back on line. The following thesis permeated the entire film: It is not technology that is dangerous, but people who do not master it. However – and this is almost sensational by Soviet standards – a scientist in front of the camera admitted that there was no one hundred percent guarantee of safety with this technology.

While the first Chernobyl film dramatically directed the deployment of the later victims at the scene of the catastrophe, now the television refrained from spectacular re-enactments of the shocking scenes. Instead – almost ten months after the accident – images from a helicopter were shown for the first time. Immediately after the disaster, the helicopter flew over the site of the fire and the radioactivity's outbreak, showing the destruction in detail with telephoto lense. The images of another life-threatening mission, which the press only reported about months later, were also shocking: Soldiers in protective clothing were sent to the edge of the burst reactor for 50 to 70 seconds at the most, in order to throw the contaminated rock down into the reactor's throat with their own hands.

The chief engineer of Chernobyl reported in front of the camera that about half of the workforce had fled. Almost all of them were men, while many women had stayed there to take care of the soldiers and helpers on disaster missions. It does seem a little strange, however, that in this film the consequences of Chernobyl are considered to have been overcome, while in the West new food contaminations are always making headlines. There is also not a single word about the possible long-term consequences of the catastrophe.

The camera shows decontamination teams at work. They wash the roofs of the high-rises in the nearby town of Pripyat; the plan is to occupy the city again. The possibly contaminated water flows over the roof down to the street. Although all other natural waters are supposedly secured, one wonders involuntarily what happens to this contaminated rinse water.

The film calls for the strictest control at work, but reduces the cause of the accident exclusively to the sloppiness of the operating personnel. The most important conclusion of Chernobyl, according to the now known position, is the realization that a nuclear war on this earth would cause incalculable damage.

JUDGMENT
IN THE CHERNOBYL TRIAL

The three main defendants in the Chernobyl trial, the director of the nuclear power plant as well as the chief engineer and his deputy, have each been sentenced to ten years in labor camps. They were sentenced to the maximum penalty for their offence provided for in Section 220, Paragraph 2 of the Ukrainian Criminal Code. The charge was based on gross violation of safety rules and criminal negligence in connection with the accident at the nuclear power plant. In addition, the director of the power plant, Viktor Bryukhanov (*1935), received an additional five-year prison sentence for abuse of office, which, however, is added to the higher sentence. Three other defendants – the shift supervisor in the fourth reactor , the supervisor on duty and a senior engineer – were sentenced to between five and two years' imprisonment.

Foreign journalists were not allowed to observe the trial themselves. Only a small selected group of Soviet correspondents could attend the trial's opening on July 7 and today's verdict. However, the Soviet press had not announced the end of the three-week trial. The Soviet media also refrained from reporting during the proceedings. Only the weekly *Moskovskiye Novosti*, which is published in five languages, had presented a major report on the trial. According to the report, serious deficiencies in the organization and safety of the nuclear power plant were identified during the negotiations.

For example, only two weeks before the catastrophe, the automatic shutdown device for a possible accident in the later exploded fourth reactor had failed; this failure had not been noted down in writing, as required. According to witnesses, the workers of the power plant did not take part in the planned qualification courses either. Urgent warnings from the Ministry of Energy to remedy existing deficiencies were ignored.

Immediately after the outbreak of the catastrophe, the director of the power plant is not even said to have ordered a radiation measurement. Neither the workers nor the population were warned at that time.

In retrospect, it turned out that the nuclear power plant did not have enough radiation measuring equipment available. Gas masks for emergency use did not exist at all. When finally, first measurement results were available, the now sentenced director Bryukhanov had prevented that these data were passed on. He finally reduced the measurement data a dozen times over vis-à-vis the authorities. In view of the court this point especially called for allegations of abuse of office. Furthermore, the court accused the director of sending in the next shift to work, without compelling necessity – this means that the workers went unprotected directly into the radioactivity.

Contrary to the early false statements in the Soviet media, the court found that the evacuation did not begin until 36 hours after the outbreak of the disaster and that a new evacuation plan had to be drawn up. Until then, neither the personnel of the power plant nor its own population had been informed.

No appeal can be lodged against the decision of the Supreme Court.

VERDICT REACHED

The people responsible for the Chernobyl breakdown have been sentenced

The criminal trial collegium of the USSR Supreme Court has named the punishment for those found guilty of the cause of the catastrophic breakdown at the nuclear power plant in Chernobyl on April 26, 1986.

Bryukhanov, the power plant's former director, has been sentenced to 10 years deprivation of freedom. Fomin, the former chief engineer, and Dyatlov, his deputy, were each also sentenced to 10 years. Rogozhkin, former shift chief, was arrested during the trial and was given five years; Kovalenko, chief of the 2nd reactor shop, was sentenced to three years, and Laushkin, former state inspector from the State Atomic Energy Inspection of the USSR, was given two years.

The sentence is not to be appealable.

Listening to the verdict are the Chernobyl plant's former director, Bryukhanov, deputy chief engineer Dyatlov and the chief engineer Fomin.

Photo by Igor KOSTIN

TO BUILD something especially for some date. To close work at least two days ahead of schedule. "To put into operation" before the clock strikes 12. And later on we'll be re-doing, re-adjusting and adding what we hadn't done at first. Only to make a report. At any price. When building something "for a date" anything goes — poor concrete and no good armature — and we'll fill in the holes later on.

be more vigilant. They remained not far from the destroyed block and got a considerable dose of radiation.

The judge and the state prosecutor are citing the radiation levels and the irradiation doses now, at the trial, nearly 18 months after the breakdown. If you learned to figure out what the instruments showed, then you'd understand what sort of terrain you were passing in the armoured car, and if you didn't learn, then you were told "It's OK!" or "We'll step on it now!" And in the first days there was even information that the radiation levels were normal. What can be achieved by such misinformation? Only, maybe, that later on people in the Ukraine and Byelorussia still didn't believe truthful and relatively good figures.

I still keep a real masterpiece, typed on the form of an organization in Kiev, signed and bearing its "out" number — everything done absolutely properly. Answering the paper a clerk writes: "The radiation situation is favourable". People did not excuse such clerks who failed to tell people that at the time it would have been better to keep the children indoors. And the advice sounded not in keeping with this when people were told that they could go back to their usual way of life, but very soon the decision was made to take the schoolchildren out of Kiev for all summer.

Today downtown Chernobyl has been put in order. The building of the House of Culture has been repaired before the trial started. A room has been set aside in it for a press centre. The square is marked in fresh white lines. And the militiamen show where arriving journalists can park their cars. Chernobyl is not like the alarmed, tense city we saw one and a half years ago, but this does not mean that no problems remain.

Deutsche Welle (West Germany) while the trial was still going on suddenly started shouting the "demand" to dock "the entire political system which bred the type of people, capable of negligence, like that which happened in Chernobyl". Everything goes as long as socialism is being denigrated. However, the trial showed the profound hypocrisy of such grudges. The atom is above political systems (isn't that what the dozens of breakdowns at the Western nuclear power plants tell us?).And it is not at all too much to know that it was a socialist system — The Union of Soviet Socialist Republics — which has condemned the negligence as it happened in Chernobyl as the gravest crime against socialist society, which is both incompatible with our idea of morality and with our laws.

There are problems with construction work and with the very status of Slavutich, the new city of power engineers. There is still oodles of work to be done on deactivating, on burying contaminated soil and structures. The people, who are working at the power plant, work in shifts. Each of these problems is a theme for a separate dialogue. Their common thing, however, is in that it is better to speak of today's problems today. In this way it will be possible to avoid new mistakes. And the old mistakes are to be as yet assessed by the open trial. The sentence in the trial that was held says: "The criminal case in respect to persons who failed to take timely measures to improve the reactor's structures, has been set aside for a special trial."

Particular desicions have been made by the court in respect to some executives from the USSR Ministry of the Power Industry and Electrification and of the Soyuzatomenergo who failed to exercise due control over the work of the station and guaranteeing its safety of operation, and also of those who failed to protect people against radiation, to organize medical service, or a service to measure the radiation danger and the town authorities will be likewise considered.

We need to always remember Chernobyl. Even when the radiation situation returns completely to normal — we must remember what led to the tragedy.

Andrei PRALNIKOV,
our special correspondent
Chernobyl

THE TRIAL, which lasted 16 separate sessions, is over. The results of examinations, testimonies of dozens of witnesses and of victims were heard, the speeches for the prosecution and for the defence were said and the accused said their last words. The sentence became the last dot, so to speak, in this affair, but it did not end the breakdown in Chernobyl.

The grief for those who died remains. The people in Pripyat and Chernobyl and tens of thousands of people in Ukrainian and Byelorussian villages will remember their evacuation their whole lives. And the area around the power plant will be known as the zone for a long time as well.

So, it is not soon that we'll be able to close the subject of Chernobyl. I'm afraid that we are speaking too little about it as it is. Much had been written about the heroism of the people who came to Chernobyl from all over the country. But the time of mass heroism is over and we shall be as yet learning the lessons of Chernobyl.

From the sentence: "A witness said that there had been quite a few violations, and that the administration was aware of them. In one case only, when he was checking on how the personnel was fulfilling the work discipline, he discovered that 12 people were fulfilling other things in their work time — playing dominoes and cards, writing letters, etc."

DURING a break in the trial someone said at the porch of the House of Culture in Chernobyl that all directors of nuclear power plants should have been invited to attend the trial. Even though the mistakes and violations, that were committed by personnel in Chernobyl and which led to the breakdown have been pointed out in great detail at all the nuclear power plants, this proposal was, probably, quite reasonable. And not only the directors but all the administrators who have something to do with the siting, building, equipping and exploiting nuclear reactors. Because there have already been breakdowns and violations at many other nuclear plants.

Stanislav Gurenko, secretary of the Central Committee of the Communist Party of the Ukraine, spoke at a recent press conference about the problems of exploitation of the Rovno plant. The lessons from its history should have been learned even earlier. It so happened that millions of roubles had to be spent strengthening the ground.

The fact that the Politbureau session of the CPSU Central Committee discussed the setting up of highly reliable automated systems of control over technological processes at nuclear power plants shows how important the problem is and the need to go over in real earnest the entire package of questions connected with atomic energy. The CPSU Central Committee and the USSR Council of Ministers have defined the complex of measures which secure the further increase of nuclear power plant safety.

The safety and reliability of nuclear power plants can be secured only by the impeccable work of all their builders and those who run them. And we can work like this — at the session of the Presidium of the USSR Academy of Sciences, devoted to Chernobyl, it was said that one of the best power plants in the world is the nuclear power plant bought from the USSR by Finland. True, the Finns did equip it with some systems and devices, but the project, the reactor and the fuel were all ours. At the session the station was called "the ideal realization of the plan". The station has also a simulator for training personnel.

From the sentence: "According to the conclusions made by the trial-technical examination, the level of technological discipline at the Chernobyl plant did not conform to the demands put to it. Systematically, there took place violations of technological rules and the generating blocks have been stopped due to the personnel's guilt. The reasons for the violations were not found out in all the cases and in separate cases the true reasons for the breakdowns were hidden. Between 1980-1986 no research was done at all in 27 cases out of 71, and many cases of equipment failure have not even been registered in the operation logs".

THE TRAINING of engineers, technicians and other operators of the power plant did not satisfy the necessary demands according to the trial-technical examination.

And this also should be a lesson. Simulators are needed. They cost a lot, but can the cost be compared to the losses caused by breakdowns? Some 100 simulators operate all over the world. But they are needed not only to train newcomers or retrain operators. During a vacation a person can lose nearly half of what he or she knows and the risks of making mistakes in an emergency situation grows.

But to date there are no simulators even in places where the training is done. The operators learn the instructions by heart and train themselves right on the job. This is instead of going through the actions on the control panel, during a breakdown imitated by an electronic computer.

From the sentence: "On December 31, 1983, in spite of the fact that the needed tests were not held at the fourth block, Bryukhanov signed the act of accepting for exploitation the starting complex on the block as if it were completed. In order to make operable the safety system, the turbogenerator was tested in 1982-1985. The tests were not good and were left unfinished. Still, Fomin, Kovalyov and Dyatlov made a technical decision and gave the order on the introduction of the conditions of run-out on the fourth generating block into experimental exploitation..."

A WITNESS said that immediately after the explosion she asked shift chief Rogozhkin what she should do? He only told her that the armed guards should not panic and that they should

goes — poor concrete and no good armature — and we'll fill in the holes later on.

We must learn this lesson properly, so that this will not be repeated either with building of housing, nor with putting a new Metro line into operation, nor with a report on an outstanding research victory.

The staff numbers at the nuclear power plant are very big. The number is being cut but still remains some three times greater than at similar foreign stations. There is the same number of operators and engineers, but the number of maintenance workers grows out of all proportion. This is explained by the fact that there is practically no item of equipment which could be put into operation without "putting it into order" — that's how our industry works. Well, and the thing "put into order" calls for keen attention later on. Even though every theoretical and practical worker knows very well that to make something work well at once is both cheaper and more beneficial. But, alas, both in the zone and at the station, already when the clean-up operation was underway, it did happen that old mistakes were repeated.

From the sentence: "Learning that the radiation level considerably exceeded the permissible level, Bryukhanov, having a vested interest — wanting to make everything seem all right in the situation that had taken shape, had hidden the fact on purpose. Abusing his power he submitted to the competent superior organizations data with lower radiation levels. The lack of broad-scale truthful information on the nature of the breakdown led to the contamination of the station personnel and of the population in the locality adjacent to the station."

COMMENT ON THE JUDGMENT IN THE CHERNOBYL TRIAL

Measured against 31 dead and 237 seriously injured, measured against damage running into billions of rubles and an uncertain future for the health of more than a hundred thousand people, the penalties in the first Chernobyl trial against those primarily responsible were mild. At any rate, this is the first impression if one wants to evaluate the ten-year prison sentence for the director of the nuclear power plant, the chief engineer and his deputy. The fact that five additional years of imprisonment were imposed on the director, which will, however, be set off against the maximum sentence, cannot diminish this impression of a mild judgement.

But this trial should not set an example. Because the boundaries for a possibly draconian punishment had already been drawn before the trial began. The public prosecutor's office formulated its accusation on the basis of an article in the Ukrainian Criminal Code which limited the maximum sentence in the present case to the ten-year imprisonment in a camp. The three other defendants, who were sentenced to between two and five years' imprisonment, also got off comparatively lightly. As shift supervisors of the exploded reactor , as supervisors on duty and as chief engineers, they were, to a certain extent, directly complicit in the emergence of the disaster.

But despite these seemingly moderate judgments, the Soviet judiciary has imposed an additional restriction – perhaps a bitter pill for those affected; for the judges who had to rule on the accused in the converted Chernobyl House of

Culture belong to the Supreme Court of the Soviet Union. Their verdict is therefore final. An appeal can no longer take place.

It seems strange, of course, that the Soviet public – as well as the foreign media – were unable to inform themselves about the course of the trial. What was basically an international affair was shielded as an internal process. The fact that a small selected group of journalists were admitted to the trial on July 7, as they are now after three weeks of trial, does not change this.

It would be desirable to know who was really on trial here. Was it just the director and his staff, was it only their personal failure or were technical deficiencies or the excessive demands on human performance discussed and evaluated? The reasons for the judgement may perhaps provide information on this, as far as they will be accessible.

There is no doubt that much blame was placed on the head of the defendants and especially on the head of the director in this trial. And if we are to believe the sole report from the initial phase of the trial that was published in a Moscow weekly newspaper, then one can only shake one's head:

The director initially refrains from taking radiation measurements at the beginning of the disaster. Then sufficient measuring instruments were lacking. There were no gas masks at all for emergency use.

The director personally withheld measurement data. And when he finally passed them on to the authorities, he reduced them a dozen times over. These many scandals were piled together on a man who was so burdened, but at the same time he took the blame for the sloppiness of the superior authorities.

So it was all his fault that wrong decisions were then made, that the population was not warned and that the evacuations were not initiated until 36 hours after the disaster began? As presumptuous as the judgment may sound from afar, the suspicion arises as if other authorities were to be washed clean, whose hesitant behavior did not exactly help to contain the catastrophe. But the final word has not yet been spoken on this trial. Further procedures are to follow.

Against the background of Soviet economic planning to quintuple nuclear power stations by the year 2000, the first Chernobyl trial, with its relatively mild verdicts, has a special function: It should not and will not unsettle other operators of nuclear power stations in the Soviet Union.

THE YEAR 1988

March 26, 1988

TWO YEARS AFTER CHERNOBYL

The second anniversary of Chernobyl was an occasion for the Soviet press to take critical stock of the catastrophe. While public awareness of the tragic accident is becoming less acute as time goes by, the big newspapers are pointing to persistent and dangerous shortcomings that could not yet be eliminated in Chernobyl.

Vladilena Abramova is the head of a scientific department set up in the Ministry of Atomic Energy following the accident to provide psychological support. Her conclusion after two years is sobering. Quote: "As a psychologist, I see the main problem in the fact that no sense of responsibility has been forthcoming among the many employees who deal with the safety of nuclear power plants". According to Ms. Abramova, the university program for the preparation of nuclear energy specialists has not in fact been changed.

The prestige of a job in a nuclear power plant has fallen considerably since Chernobyl, with the result that less and less qualified people are signing up for this work.

Nevertheless, Chernobyl itself has set up two scientifically supervised training centers in which all conceivable accident situations are played out. According to the latest information, all Chernobyl personnel have already been trained in these centers.

The *Pravda* criticism on this anniversary, which reports a lack of control and analysis during the repair work at the nuclear power station, must be taken all the more seriously. The party newspaper had accused the responsible ministry of tolerating gross mistakes and miscalculations in Chernobyl.

In another report the Ukrainian Prime Minister Vitaliy Masol (1928-2018) points out that in the past two years almost eleven thousand houses have been built for the evacuees. The decontamination work in the affected areas has not yet been completed.

The evacuees have to come to terms with the fact that all the furniture and appliances in the fifteen thousand contaminated apartments in Pripyat are now being destroyed because, according to the government newspaper *Izvestia*, they are threatening to become a source of the epidemic danger. Elsewhere, the paper reports that decontamination actions even had to be repeated in isolated cases because radioactive deposits had again been detected during follow-up measurements.

Nevertheless, according to the latest data, workers at the nuclear power plant are only exposed to about one third of the permissible annual dose of radioactivity. The filter systems on a newly constructed extraction duct in the nuclear power plant, according to the plant director in his inspection sheet, had remained completely clean even after a quarterly operation.

VISIT TO CHERNOBYL

The way from Kiev to Chernobyl leads through a blossoming Ukrainian spring landscape and ends in the desert. An eight inches (20 cm) thick, contaminated layer of earth was removed for miles around the nuclear power plant and filled with fresh sand.

The liquidators at work. One can see that the contaminated soil from the surface has been removed.

The trees of the forests near by were destroyed by the radiation and have now been cut down. A few authorized correspondents were allowed to visit the power station in the spring of 1988, two years after the catastrophe. We journalists get the feeling that we are surrounded by total desolation.

Without waiting for our questions, Alexander Kovalenko, the head of the information department at the nuclear power station, right away began to enumerate the worst shortcomings in connection with the disaster:

During the salvage work immediately after the disaster, there had been disputes over competence, because forty different ministries at the regional and federal level, were involved and each had a say in the matter.

Finally, a special working group was set up to eliminate the damage; it was professionally organized without dispute over jurisdiction.

"You have five minutes to visit the sarcophagus," warned the spokesman for the power station and pressed a measuring instrument into my hand. This allowed me to venture up to about 220 yards to the burst ruins of the reactor , which was surrounded by a skin of lead and actually resembled a sarcophagus. Depending on the direction of the wind, the Geiger counter erratically jumped from level to level.

The ruin of the accident fourth reactor , called the "Sarcophagus", was transformed into an almost square concrete surrounded by thick lead walls. The first floors of the fifth and sixth reactor s stand not far away as unfinished construction sides. Until the year 1991 further building may not be continued any longer.[45] But the nuclear power plant itself is allegedly "working normally" and the new director proudly presents the latest statistics. "Production is above target."

In the meantime, another ten thousand people work in the exclusion zone, which has a diameter of about thirty

---

[45] After the end of the Soviet Union in December 1991 the Republic of Ukraine decided not to finish building these two reactor s. In the meantime, the complete nuclear power plant of Chernobyl has been shut down as of the year 2000.

kilometers (18 miles), but even two years after the accident, the skilled workers are still only on duty for 15 days. After that, they have to take another 15 days off. None of them live in the restricted zone. Buses take them from a nearby settlement to work.

A visit to the Chernobyl nuclear power plant
two years after the explosion.

According to the plant management, "the job applications for work in Chernobyl are now very high again". As a special benefit for new workers, there is an offer of an apartment for the family in Kiev and double the salary.

The inner district around the power station and the evacuated town of Pripyat is surrounded by a fence that triggers signals when touched. The return of the inhabitants to this area is unthinkable. A bus brings us to this place Pripyat, from which 50 thousand people had to be evacuated. In front of us there are spraying-trucks, which clean the already decontaminated road again from radioactive dust.

We journalists are forbidden to get out of our bus. But we see the shattered windows through which the furniture of the apartments was hurled out. From the 10 to 20-story skyscrapers, decontamination teams had thrown the apartment contents through the windows onto the streets and then "buried" it in the radiation zone. When asked whether the people had lost everything, a representative of the nuclear power plant said:

"Before the final destruction of the furniture, one person per family was allowed to come and secure the most important documents. Of course, everything was under the protection of experts who had decontaminated this person as well as all the objects he wanted to take out of the contaminated zone."

At the edge and even within this 30-kilometer (18 miles) zone, however, almost five hundred old people have returned to their villages. The Chernobyl Control Commission wants to leave them there and declares that even more settlements are habitable again. However, new cities are now being built for the evacuees, some of which offer considerably more comfort than the old settlements.

At a conference in Kiev on the medical aspects of the nuclear accident, the latest figures on the follow-up costs to date were presented: According to these figures, the Soviet Union had to invest the equivalent of about 10.5 billion US dollars in Chernobyl, half of which was spent on technical repairs and new safety measures alone.

At the end of the conference in Kiev, which was attended by scientists from two dozen countries, there were clear differences in the assessment of medical aspects. The majority of Soviet physicians tend not to make projections nor do they reveal any clinical specifics of illnesses due to radiation.

Some Soviet scientists, but above all the American physician Dr. Robert Gale, who was very committed to the radiation victims, demanded a projection as accurate as possible for the next 50 years in order to be able to counter the rampant rumors, especially in Kiev. Despite a so far unusually open scientific discussion, it became however clear how insufficient all past data have been, in order to draw real conclusions for the health burden of the population.

The liquidators at work.

THE YEAR 1989

February 22, 1989

GORBACHEV IN CHERNOBYL

A full evening program on Soviet television with Mikhail Gorbachev: The news program *Vremya*, usually 30 minutes long, was extended to two hours and 15 minutes for the Party Leader. The occasion was a keynote speech by Gorbachev in Kiev with critical remarks on the slow progress of *perestroika* and his visit to Chernobyl.

There, in Chernobyl, Gorbachev stood in the first reactor of the nuclear power plant, wearing a white coat and cap, and had the shift supervisor explain to him what was going on. The party leader always interrupted when safety issues were at stake. Did the new automatic system really work? Is it now possible to rule out mistakes? Then Gorbachev got into conversation with the workers of the nuclear power plant. Their concerns: shortcomings in medical care. And the Soviet press, they complained, was polemicizing against nuclear energy inaccurately.

Gorbachev then acted as the advocate of the public. Quote: "In some ways you need to understand the press. The public concerns, the distrust are justified."

In the newly built city of Slavutych where Chernobyl employees are now housed, the party leader then taught a lesson in nuclear energy in front of the camera using the methods of a senior teacher. He called on experts to explain in a few sentences what's bothering them and what they expect from nuclear energy.

The Chernobyl plant director asked for more qualified attention from the mass media and praised nuclear power as "the cleanest thing we have ecologically". The chief scientist Yevgeny Velikhov saw no chance to cover the Soviet energy demand without nuclear power and stated that society has to adapt to it.

The politician Ukrainian Boris Shcherbina, head of the then Catastrophe Commission, simply said: "Young people must learn to observe regulations better so that an accident like Chernobyl does not repeat itself."

Environmental chief Yuri Izrael confirmed that it would be possible to live in parts of the restricted zone again if only certain types of mushrooms were not allowed to be eaten there.

Gorbachev himself was the only one in front of the camera who still reflected on the disaster and its consequences.

"I consider it my duty to be here," he said, calling for a greater sense of responsibility in dealing with nuclear energy.

But there were no valid references to recent publications on the dramatic consequences of radiation sickness in the Chernobyl catchment area.

Meanwhile, under the pressure of worried public opinion, the first reactor unit of Armenia's only nuclear power plant is being shut down today. In mid-March, the operation of this nuclear power plant is to be completely shut down in order to convert it into a thermal power plant at a later date.

April 26, 1989

CHERNOBYL –
THREE YEARS AFTER

The Soviet Union is still working on overcoming the Chernobyl accident. And this, in two ways:

The first is to respond to public concerns about nuclear energy. Since the accident, new voices have been raised calling for a critical debate on nuclear energy, in particular, the accelerated expansion of which is being pursued by Soviet economic planning.

Secondly, however, experts must eliminate existing and identifiable risks that have been demonstrated in the practice of Soviet nuclear power stations to date. This applies above all to the Chernobyl reactor type, which will no longer be built in the future. The concrete consequence of this is the decision that the two other planned reactor units at Chernobyl will not be completed either. However, the interruption of construction work after the accident made it clear early on that work on the existing new ruins would hardly be resumed.

In addition, two nuclear power plants in Smolensk and Kursk, using the same technology as the Chernobyl nuclear power plant, have already been shut down. Nationwide, all units of the same type built in the 1970s are to be modernized and equipped with further safety precautions.

At the same time, the Soviet Union is continuing their roadmap to shut down certain reactor units completely.

This year and next year, for example, this will apply to reactor units in the Beloyarsk and Novovoronezh nuclear power plants.

The only nuclear power plant operated in Armenia in the immediate vicinity of the capital Yerevan has since been completely shut down following the severe earthquake in December 1988. The concerns of the population are seen as the main reason for this step.

Parallel to these measures, the Soviet government is trying to reassure the public with a new information policy. Nuclear power stations are now open for regular visits: Company representatives, training centers, public organizations – all of them are now to be given a kind of on-site demonstration of nuclear energy. In addition, an information center for nuclear energy has been established in Moscow and public discussions on nuclear energy are regularly held in a specialized institute.

Nevertheless, considerable difficulties remain, particularly in dealing with the consequences of Chernobyl. This was again made clear at the end of March by a publication in the party newspaper *Pravda*. The responsible minister Izrael explained on an entire newspaper page the problems of the still effective radioactive contamination. For illustration purposes, *Pravda* printed three maps from the Chernobyl catchment area, in which detailed measurements of the contamination were recorded. In his conclusion, the expert spoke of "the fact that radioactive contamination of the environment in a considerable area still represents a serious technical and social problem".

The visit of party leader Gorbachev to Chernobyl at the end of February this year was of a demonstrative nature in view of the still deep concern among the population.

The weekly *Moskovskiye Novosti* had reported[46] on the real catastrophic long-term consequences, which are only now beginning to emerge, just slightly later after Gorbachev's appearance in Chernobyl.

A reporter had visited a collective farm in the catchment area of the radioactive contamination. A frightening increase

---

[46] see footnote 18.

in malformations was noted in the livestock breeding there. The report concerning about 440 head of cattle reads:

"In the five years before Chernobyl altogether three cases of physical abnormalities among the piglets were registered. There were none among the calves at all.

But already within the first year after the accident, 64 malformed animals were born. 37 piglets and 27 calves were born without heads and extremities, eyes or ribs".

Among the human population the number of miscarriages more than doubled. According to the newspaper, 76 cases were registered in the two years following the catastrophe. And these figures come only from a single collective farm in a more distant region of the disaster area.

Such publications are unsettling above all for women, who are pregnant or want to become pregnant. The responsible Ministry of Health in Kiev has long maintained the statement that there is no longer any danger outside the immediate Chernobyl radiation zone.

"If there is no longer any danger, as we are repeatedly told", the weekly newspaper *Moskovskiye Novosti* quoted one affected woman, "why are we advised against pregnancy?"

Finally, the paper referred to a representative of the local administration in the Zhitomir area, which lies far outside the so-called danger zone. According to him, the medical staff has noticed a significant increase in chronic illnesses. It is said that recovery times are getting longer and longer after surgical interventions. And further, literally: "Also, the annual average of cancer cases has doubled – above all, we have noticed this in lip and mouth cancer."

30 YEARS LATER – LOOKING BACK

alpha-Forum[47]
Presented by the moderator Carolin Nyhuis

Moderator: I would like to welcome you to today's *alpha-Forum*, which will focus on "30 Years of Chernobyl". I am looking forward very much to my guest today, Dr. Johannes Grotzky. He is a journalist, former BR Radio Director, Eastern Europe expert, Honorary Professor at the University of Bamberg and he was the ARD[48] Correspondent in Moscow from 1983 to 1989. It is precisely at this time that I would like to talk to him today, because it was during this time that the Chernobyl nuclear disaster occurred.

On April 26, 1986, Chernobyl suffered the greatest catastrophe in the history of civilian nuclear energy use. Do you remember exactly when and how you heard about it?

Grotzky: Oh yes! Not from Soviet sources – we didn't hear about it in the Soviet Union. No, I got a phone call. It was RIAS-Berlin[49] and I was told they had a report that there was some radioactive cloud registered in Sweden; and there was a suspicion that this cloud came from Eastern Europe, and if I

---

[47] Presented on German TV April 26, 2016, 8:15-9:00 p.m. on the *ARD-alpha* Channel. Original text retrieved August 5, 2019 under
https://www.br.de/fernsehen/ard-alpha/sendungen/alpha-forum/
johannes-grotzky-sendung-100.html
[48] ARD – The German Public Radio & TV Network.
[49] RIAS – Radio in the American Sector of Berlin, retrieved June 1, 2020 under
https://en.wikipedia.org/wiki/Rundfunk_im_amerikanischen_Sektor

knew anything about whether the Soviet Union might be involved. I replied that, firstly, I do not know anything about it and, secondly, I do not believe it. But I was still unsure, because at the beginning of my work in the Soviet Union I had already received such a strange phone call in early September of 1983. At that time, a radio colleague called me from West Germany saying:

"Look, – some passenger plane from South Korea must have disappeared somewhere there in the Soviet Union".

I reacted almost jokingly: "Do you think my Russian friends shot down this plane?" –

Actually, it had really been shot down! By a Soviet fighter plane. And that was kept secret for eight days.

But in 1986 we had a different situation: Gorbachev had already been in office for a year and there had been a major Party Congress a month before the Chernobyl catastrophe. This Party Congress was supposed to be the starter for *glasnost* and *perestroika:* Gorbachev actually wanted to give the starting signal that everything should now be opened up and that from now on the country really wants to deal critically with all the things that have to be changed. That's why I said: "If something had really happened, then information would have to come immediately from the Soviet side".

But that didn't happen.

Moderator: When exactly did you hear about it? On the same day, April 26?

Grotzky: No, not at all. We only officially heard about it when a TASS message came in: That was about 48 hours later in the news program *Vremya*, that is, on the evening of April 28. There was a four-line report with the content that there had been an accident, that a government commission had been set up and that efforts had been made to eliminate the consequences of the accident. It was not said exactly what had happened. But gradually the floodgates were opened. In Moscow, nobody really knew what had occurred. And only later did we learn, that 600 miles away in Chernobyl a mere test run had been done on a reactor. If I may briefly explain this rather simple story – in reality, of course, it is much more complicated and there are also minute-by-minute protocols to this accident, because experts have really worked through everything in these three decades: In the end, it was the case that a test was to be made on reactor 4, that had previously been done on reactor 3. But already at reactor 3 the test had gone wrong. They had wanted to find out what happens when the reactor is shut down, when no electricity is supplied to the reactor for operation, i.e. when there is no electricity from outside. They wanted to know whether the turbines within the reactor would still start anyway or whether the turbines would have enough energy to start the diesel engines that were available to ensure cooling. This was actually a safety check and it started on April 25, one o'clock in the morning, i.e. the reactor was slowly shut down from then on. But then the shutdown was interrupted because the city of Kiev said: "Stop! Stop! We need energy, you can't suddenly stop Kiev's energy supply!" This nuclear power plant was relatively new; it was only about three years old.

Therefore, they moved the security check to the following night on April 26. When the reactor was shut down that night, a terrible first mistake happened, as one could reconstruct in the meantime. A technician obviously entered the wrong number, because the reactor was only allowed to be lowered to 20 percent of its capacity. As far as we know, the reactor registered one percent instead of 20. Either the technician made a mistake or there was something wrong with the machine he was working on – and to this day it has not been possible to find out exactly what happened. Finally, the reactor was reduced to one percent of its capacity. In the chain reaction that followed, the situation became more and more uncontrollable:

Turbine controls were handled incorrectly, cooling systems were switched off. Heat increased markedly, so fuel rods bent and could no longer be handled properly. In the end, there was this rapid heating effect to 3,600 degrees Fahrenheit. What then happened was what everyone became aware of later – but the local population was able to see it directly: The resulting explosion blew up the 1,000-ton concrete ceiling above the reactor along with the outer weather protection roof. A cloud of fire about 1,100 meters (1,200 yards) was reported to have developed above the reactor.

The really dramatic thing was that for ten days, radioactivity was blown out of this hole, out of this reactor, which was open at the top, into the air. During these ten days, there was a delay of 36 hours before people were evacuated from the immediate vicinity of this reactor.

Moderator: This means that you could not get upset at first when you heard about this matter, because it was simply not yet clear what the extent of this disaster would be.

Grotzky: You know, of course we had a different attitude. At the time we said, "Well, what the West is bringing us now in terms of information or possible suspicions is always a bit exaggerated." Back then, people simply liked to make the incidents that occurred in the Soviet Union a little bigger from the outside – but within the Soviet Union they made them a little smaller every time. So we thought that this might not be true after all. We phoned around and, of course, tried to get direct information from the area affected. I could already imagine that there might be something to this story, but I had no idea about the real extent.

We just had no idea about what had happened. And nothing was reported from Kiev or Chernobyl either, but first they said: "Everything's fine!" And the party headquarters in Kiev had not even reported anything to Moscow. In this respect, many people in Moscow really did not know what was going on. Even Gorbachev, whom I asked about it later, told me quite honestly, no, he didn't know what had really happened until about 30 hours later.

Moderator: Let's listen to the first report that you made as an ARD correspondent in Moscow at noon on April 29, three days later. This is a report that – you say today –you were incredibly confused because you really had no information at all. Let's listen to it.

Radio broadcast April 29, 1986, Grotzky reporting:
"The reports from the accident area are few. Some correspondents have been able to telephone with the Ukrainian capital Kiev, which lies about 80 miles south of Chernobyl. According to this information there is no exceptional situation in Kiev. The city is said to be quiet and there is supposedly no evidence of evacuation measures. Moscow embassies, which have a consular mission in Kiev, have received similar information. On the outskirts of Kiev, the staff of a German company, which has contacted the Moscow Foreign Ministry via the German embassy, is working to obtain possible rules of conduct in the event of a disaster. A reaction from the Foreign Ministry is not yet available."

Grotzky: If I may pick up on that right now, because there are a lot of strange things hidden in this report.

The first point is that we journalists were all unsure how to pronounce this place. In the *Soviet Encyclopedia*, the pronunciation reference to "Chernobyl" says that the emphasis is on the last syllable, which was allegedly wrong. I have pronounced the word "'Chérnobyl" in this report with the emphasis on the first syllable. But the real pronunciation – I asked that again in Ukraine – is "'Chernóbyl" with the emphasis on the "o". So we did not even know how to pronounce this place: we simply did not know it.

The second point was that we had no information and no informants. Of course we tried to find out what happened, we tried to talk to people. We also couldn't observe anything, because none of us could get as far as the power station itself or the town of Pripyat. There were about 50,000 people living in Pripyat, near Chernobyl, workers and their families residing nearby this nuclear power station. Of these 50,000 people, 15,000 were children. All these people were not informed at first. After 36 hours, these people were told that they would have to leave their homes for three days because some cleaning work had to be carried out. Of course, these people never came back – except for a few, which I only learned later when I myself was in Chernobyl and Pripyat two and a half years later.

Moderator: Today it is of course absolutely unimaginable that one has no or so little information and can only report about it three days later. Today, there would probably be more than 50 messages with pictures via Twitter, Facebook, etc. immediately afterwards.

You say that the Soviet Union has always played down the catastrophes in its own country; but bad news from abroad, even if banal, has been a integral part of Soviet TV programs. How do you explain that? Why was that so?

Grotzky: Of course, the inner view was that the country had to be described as successful. But that also resulted in a lot of very bitter jokes. On television, for example, people have always shown how early the harvest is brought in and how big it was again this year. In reality, Gorbachev said at the Party Congress immediately before this catastrophe that 30 percent of the harvests actually rot in the fields every year and how bad the agricultural sector is. But on television there has always been talk of huge and early harvests. Smiling, my friends always said: "We are already bringing in next year's harvest today - that's how early we are in fulfilling the plan". And at Chernobyl these comments immediately started to get slightly ironic, because the drama simply hadn't been recognized yet. They said: "There is no such thing as radioactivity! Besides, it is sinking constantly!"

It was clear to everyone that there was something behind the news that people were not told. You really had to read the news between the lines. And it is true that the catastrophes that happened abroad were always presented much bigger than they really were. I also remember the instructions to my Soviet TV colleagues who worked in Germany at the time. They were given two guidelines: They were never allowed to film the large amount of products and goods offered in any department stores or shops; and, in particular, they were also not allowed to show in their reports many of these beautiful luxury cars that were driving around in Germany. Instead, they had the task of showing where the social hotspots and problems of Germany lie. So, when reports from Germany were broadcast on Soviet television, one saw mainly the problem of unemployment, or Sinti and Roma who had to live in some settlements, or people begging in the streets, etc. That was definitely a very clear distortion of reality. Conversely, the Soviet Union accused us Western correspondents of the same thing saying, "You are no different!" And that was true of Chernobyl, because some Western newspapers insisted in "unconfirmed reports" of up to 15,000 dead as a result of the accident. But that was incorrect.

The USA did play an important role in this whole story, which we are less aware of today. There were two Americans who had immediately come to Moscow when it became clear what had actually happened.

One person was Robert Gale. I noticed this interesting man because he always walked around in clogs without socks. He is an immunologist, microbiologist and doctor and had developed a treatment of bone marrow transplants and immediately offered his help. He flew to Moscow with a complete team and with comprehensive technical equipment and then took care of all those people who were the first victims of the radiation.

The second man was Armand Hammer, who we really don't remember today either. He was an entrepreneur and head of a large oil company and was the son of an immigrant from old Odessa, who also remained a socialist in the USA. Armand Hammer was an active Capitalist Communist with an American passport and had even negotiated with Lenin himself in his first transactions in the Soviet Union. For many decades he did business with the Soviet Union as an American. He also came to Moscow immediately and brought with him large quantities of medicine from the USA, which he had paid for himself.

These two then had a meeting with Gorbachev. They were in Moscow for a few days and always kept themselves informed; Gale commuted constantly between the USA and the Soviet Union during this time. Later I attended a conference with him in Ukraine. During a private conversation I learned a great deal from Dr. Gale. According to Dr. Gale, Gorbachev told him and Hammer at their meeting: "I thank you for your help in this disaster. However, far worse for me is what you have done in the USA with your negative reports and campaigns against our Soviet Union!"

But in public, Gorbachev himself – and this is the interesting thing – this man, who stood for *glasnost* and *perestroika*, was nowhere to be seen.

Then, it all started in the newspapers, followed by reports on television. There were the first films of the helicopter operations, which were throwing all kinds of material into the damaged roof of the reactor: boron and cement and lead and so on. They just wanted to cover this hole again with all their might. They didn't know at all what exactly had happened, but they knew they couldn't extinguish the fire with water and sand.

Gorbachev had still not shown up in public. Only 18 days later he appeared on television with a speech that shocked us all. Because, in this speech he said that the really bad thing was not Chernobyl, but what the USA and the Federal Republic of Germany made of it. That was, so to speak, the low point of his relationship with the Federal Republic, because in

Germany there was indeed a great deal of excitement about this catastrophe and of course the media reported constantly about it. The Federal Republic was indeed more affected by the radioactive fallout than, for example, Moscow. But we did not know all that at the time. We were all just in panic.

Gorbachev presented it all in this way and complained to Robert Gale, the American doctor, and to the American entrepreneur Armand Hammer, how awful it was that foreign countries were making even more of a fuss than necessary. Then he combined that with his proposal to disarm nuclear weapons, which was another topic entirely. At this time in his foreign policy, Gorbachev demanded: "Away with all nuclear weapons!" And in domestic affairs he insisted: "Away with all political pressure!" The Party Congress before Chernobyl had already stated: "This generation will not live in Communism. We are not able to achieve such goals."

One year later at a Party Conference Gorbachev was more radical, announcing: "The political system of the Soviet Union has failed!" This formulation was really the direct consequence of Chernobyl.

Moderator: But it has to be said that Gorbachev was not yet President but Secretary-General at that time.

Grotzky: He was the Party Leader.

Moderator: Exactly.

Grotzky: That was a bit complicated. At that time, Gorbachev was Chairman of the Party, i.e. Chairman of the Politburo. In addition, he then became Chairman of the Supreme Soviet. So he was the head of state after all. But you're right, these two functions were separate at the time, because he himself only introduced a presidential constitution later and finally became the first and last President of the Soviet Union.

Moderator: Let's return briefly to the point under which you had to work as a journalist at the time. At first you didn't get any information. In the beginning, you might have thought that this could also be due to the fact that it took place in an area where you couldn't travel too easily; that's why you didn't get any information at first. But when did you realize that there was actually a non-information policy behind it?

Grotzky: Well, we had already prepared ourselves very early on for the fact that the information policy of the old Soviet Union consisted of concealing the truth. And if you conceal the truth, you don't necessarily lie. However, the example of the shooting down of a South-Korean airplane that I mentioned earlier influenced me a great deal with regard to Soviet information policy. At that time, the Soviet press spokesman was Leonid Zamyatin, and this Mr. Zamyatin once really verbally attacked a German television colleague in front of everybody at an international press conference in Moscow. It was about this terrible case, the shooting down of this South Korean plane. The German correspondent Lutz Lehmann had asked: "Why didn't you tell us eight days ago when it happened, instead of lying to us all the time?"

Zamyatin replied: "If you react like this, you neither understand us, nor our language. We have never lied! "

In fact, they did not lie, but said: "A plane of foreign origin entered Soviet airspace and disappeared in the direction of the Sea of Japan."

The fact that it had been shot down and crashed, remained unsaid. But what they said wasn't a lie. And again, in the case of Chernobyl, the information policy was the same. Those were the old conservative party members accusing Gorbachev of revealing to much and exposing the country with his policy of *glasnost*. Obviously, there must have been a power struggle, that also took place in the Politburo. As a result, it seems *Pravda* had been given the green light, and also television could start reporting on Chernobyl. That basically took about a week, and it can be said that the first major reports were already running in mid-May. By the end of May, practically all the dramatic reports were available.

This information policy increased step by step. On the first anniversary of the disaster, parents held their children, who had been born with deformities due to radiation, in front of the television cameras and accused the state of not really doing anything for them. Relatively soon other details became known: There were cows born with two heads, there were other malformed animals on farms near Chernobyl. All this was made public relatively quickly in the course of the following months.

The problem for us Western journalist was that we couldn't make free telephone calls. If we wanted to make private calls, we had to register the call 24 hours in advance; if we wanted to make business calls, about two hours ahead. Imagine our news desk in Germany! They say, in my case: "We want to have you on the air right after the news at twelve noon German time." I then said: "Well, after twelve noon means for us journalists working in the Soviet Union that we need to order a telephone line between twelve noon and 2 p.m. German time. But we never know when we will be connected by the Soviet operator within this time slot."

So we had to react quite differently. We could not report events as they happened like Twitter and Instagram do today. The second problem was that we were not allowed to travel freely within the Soviet Union. That's also something we tend to forget today. As I mentioned, we couldn't make free phone calls, couldn't dial and call on our own, because every call had to be registered and arranged by the Soviet authorities. Of course, we had to take into account, that our calls would be bugged. Often the "dear people, who were taking care of us", even interrupted the broadcast. That's why I always said: "Anyone who came to the Soviet Union as a non-believer quickly becomes a believer, because he soon learns that a higher being hears and sees everything."

So that was the first thing, and the second was: we couldn't travel. I couldn't say, "I'm going to Kiev now." A trip had to be registered and approved 48 hours in advance. And of course you also needed someone official from the Soviet side who took care of you during the trip, because as a foreign journalist you were not allowed to travel alone. These were all restrictions under which we suffered. Today we are often told: "My God, how did you report back then?! Couldn't you have done more?" No, that was not possible due to the working conditions.

The other thing was that we lived in a kind of isolated community. The foreigners lived together and were therefore able to inform each other from foreign news sources. Inside the Soviet Union, on the other hand, there were mostly rumors. When the radioactivity from Chernobyl became known, many good Russian friends told me: "There is only one remedy: drink vodka! That's the only thing that helps against it." That's what the rumors were like.

Moderator: You said that although there were no direct lies, these things were deliberately played down. There were also the experts who were consulted, and the ministries in Kiev then released various statements that really played down the whole thing, while everything else was described as spreading panic. In disaster reporting, isn't it always a balancing act between creating panic on the one hand and information and clarification on the other?

Grotzky: That's always the case. Let's take a look at a current event. In India there are always accidents in which hundreds of people die. For the Western media, however, this is only a side note. Back in Moscow, when one person got crushed to death in the subway, we had a big headline in the West. The news was always tied to what political relationship we had with each other: Is that a political opponent? Then his catastrophe is always greater than mine. Is that a political friend? Then you have to react with compassion. That was, I believe, the classic reporting scheme in this East-West relationship.

On the other hand, the Soviet Union had not handled the situation well at that time. It was not only the case that many mistakes were made in Chernobyl itself: The experts list seven specific mistakes that led to this disaster. In addition, there were the communication errors. But beyond that, the Soviet Union did not do what it should have done, namely to report immediately to the International Atomic Energy Agency (IAEA) in Vienna. It had allowed quite some time to pass before it did so. The head of the IAEA in Vienna, Hans Blix, got in touch with Moscow and asked what was going on there. He was then invited to the Soviet Union to visit Chernobyl. There he flew by helicopter over the power plant and then gave a press conference. In other words, he sat down with us, with the correspondents. Next, he did something that irritated us. – He was, as one might say, "the supreme lobbyist for nuclear energy in the world". – He said that this was an accident, but that it would be brought under control and that there was no reason why we should not continue to focus on nuclear energy and develop it further. Two worlds really clashed together here.

The Soviet Union had put the world's first nuclear power plant into operation many years before[50] – which we have already forgotten   and then continued to expand nuclear energy. There are well-known reactors like RBMK etc.; some of them are allegedly less safe than others. But one thing is clear: The former Soviet Union and today's Russia have continuously relied on nuclear energy, as has France, for example. Much of the energy needed for the country is supplied by nuclear power. In other words, nuclear energy as such has hardly been called into question. In the course of the events at Chernobyl, however, a female politician from

---

[50] On June 27, 1954, the world's first nuclear power station to generate electricity for a power grid, the Obninsk Nuclear Power Plant, started operations in Obninsk, in the Soviet Union. Retrieved June 7, 2020 under https://en.wikipedia.org/wiki/Nuclear_power_plant

Germany came to Moscow: Jutta Ditfurth, who hardly anyone knows today. She was a founding member of the Green Party. She brought these famous stickers and buttons, "Atomic power? No thanks!", in a Russian translation, and tried to distribute them, but found no response at all. In other words, even after Chernobyl, it was not nuclear energy as such that was discredited in Soviet society, but the management of this accident was discredited, the management of how people were treated.

On the other hand, there was an extreme solidarity, which is already very surprising. In the end, hundreds of thousands of so-called "liquidators" came to Chernobyl and did some cleaning work there. They tried to help. The evacuations had taken place, i.e. these people had to be accommodated somewhere. About two and a half years later I had the opportunity to go there with Dr. Robert Gale and others. I had experiences that made me very thoughtful, that made me very insecure. I still don't know how to deal with it. The first experience was the following: The people who looked after me, who were working there, told me that nobody wanted to slaughter all the cattle back then; therefore, the animals were brought outside this 30-kilometer (18 miles) zone to the surrounding collective farms. The argument was: "If there is cesium in the milk, then it is mixed with the other, non-contaminated milk in such a way that the level of radiation from this cesium is no longer dangerous for the consumers". I was officially told that and I still have all these recordings.

The second experience was that I was taken to Pripyat. This place looked devastated at that time. First of all, I noticed the amount of destruction of the apartments themselves and inquired about them. I got the answer: "Yes, there have been looters in the last two years and they have plundered these apartments". That is, the things that had been stolen from these contaminated apartments were then sold on the black market. However, the worst thing was that the evacuees were allowed to return to their homes in the first week after the accident, one family member per family, in order to collect the most important documents from their apartments. So people were once again allowed to return to this highly contaminated zone. No one really knew how serious the consequences were. To this day, I am completely stunned by this.

The third drastic experience I had at that time was when I took photos there myself. We weren't allowed to take many photos, but there are still three photos left from back then. The entire surface soil around Chernobyl had been removed. I really came into a desert there: Although not within the entire radius of 18 miles, but several miles around the damaged power station, the entire topsoil had been removed – and nothing had grown by then. In the meantime, of course, there are plants there again. In addition, they tried to dump everything that stood outside, i.e. all the cars etc., into large pits, because they were all completely contaminated. Later the helicopters and the trucks were also thrown into these pits. Why the helicopters? The helicopters had been used to pour all the material into this open hole from above, to seal this radiated reactor core. Of course all these helicopters were also completely contaminated.

The dramatic thing at that time was that they didn't have enough helicopters; therefore, they had to take them away from the Soviet army fighting in Afghanistan and bring them about three thousand miles to Chernobyl. This was a flight time of 20 hours per helicopter. After being used in Chernobyl, of course, they were completely contaminated. As a result, huge pits were needed to bury all this. However, they could not always be guarded. These areas were also plundered and many of these contaminated items – even helicopter parts – were then sold on the black market.

Moderator: You mentioned Pripyat: Almost 50,000 inhabitants lived in this city and most of them also worked in this nuclear power plant. Where were all these people evacuated to? There was also a need for workers who then erected this ceiling, this sarcophagus.

Grotzky: There were many people who came from outside for this purpose. One must not forget that some of the responsible staff, i.e. chief engineers, deputy directors, etc. fled immediately after the disaster. In this emergency, they left everything behind and ran away. Many people came from outside and I also had contact with doctors who helped there and who told me about the terrible consequences of this disaster. They told me that of course there were many, many more fatalities and that one had to expect that all this would become even more terrible in the next few years.

So on the one hand people ran away; then many others came from outside who really helped heroically and risked their lives – and unfortunately sacrificed it often enough. One could accommodate the people at that time only in surrounding collective and state farms; relatively fast a new town with the name Slavutych was then established. This is a replacement town for Pripyat; it is outside the 30 kilometer (18 miles) zone. This 30 kilometer zone was thus taboo and everybody had to leave it – except for those workers, who were allowed only hourly into this zone. Directly after the explosion, within the actual area of reactor four, the emergency crews were only allowed to work for about 40 seconds. These workers were brought by helicopters up onto the roof. They then shoveled – for forty seconds – as much debris as possible into the hole and were quickly taken away by the hovering helicopters. In addition, others had to decontaminate the undamaged parts of the roof with cleansing agents.

The people who did this were actually deployed at one-minute-intervals until they received the highest radiation dose that was barely acceptable. Then they were taken out from there. That's why they came up with such a high total of 600,000 people who were deployed there during the course of this accident. Because some of the liquidators who worked there were so severely contaminated in a matter of seconds that they had to get out right away. That was one situation, i.e. there were many workers' camps surrounding this 30 kilometer zone.

The other matter was that into this 30 km zone some weeks after the evacuation quite a few people went back. Later, I visited this zone and met these people myself. These were people who did not live in Pripyat, but in small villages within this zone. Even then – with the high radiation levels – they continued to live in their old homes, sometimes with terrible consequences. But those were mainly old people who simply wanted to live out their lives there. Of course I asked those responsible why they allowed that to happen. They replied to me: "What should we do? These people were already completely contaminated and are even more so now. They know that they will soon die. So let us simply let them live in their old, very, very simple huts." Unfortunately, many, many sad life stories came to an end in this way, about which no one talked any more.

It was only later that some photographers made long-term documentaries of these people: They showed what dramatic consequences this catastrophe really had for the villagers there. We still do not know the actual number of victims. There are people who speak of many tens of thousands of deaths as a result of this disaster, some even of hundreds of thousands. Others, on the other hand, say that in the end there were only a few hundred deaths. But we will never know for sure.

Moderator: You spoke about these photographers. Did you know Igor Kostin? Did you talk to this photographer with his first pictures of Chernobyl?

Grotzky: No, I didn't know him. He really brought out the first photos. The radiation was so strong that even the negatives were affected by it. He also kept some photos for himself, which were published much later. And in the beginning, there were hardly any pictures made public. But there is something else: There was already satellite reconnaissance! However, at that time, our American friends were not ready to communicate their findings to the public. My interpretation then was, that none of the officials in America wanted to turn this accident in Chernobyl against the development of nuclear energy itself. Perhaps there was also an American interest at the time in saying: "We don't want to play this up too much so that we don't end up with a movement against nuclear energy".

Moderator: In your opinion, was that also the reason why the Soviet Union kept this catastrophe so small in the beginning?

Grotzky: No. Nuclear energy has never been questioned in the Soviet Union or Russia. We really have to be clear about that. This was simply an accident. For many it was something like a punishment from God, just as many people in the country also felt that Gorbachev himself was God's punishment, too. That Gorbachev was seen this way, we did not perceive in the West; we could not and did not want to see him in such a way. Gorbachev has this birthmark on top of his forehead: People I knew in the Soviet Union often portrayed it to me as "the mark of the devil". For these people Gorbachev was a man who was sent to their country as punishment. He is also the most unpopular politician in Russia today, as you should know, because he is "the man who destroyed the Soviet Union". This is in stark contrast to Gorbachev's popularity in Germany at this time.

I was also repeatedly told about Chernobyl: "This is an act of God! It's meant to teach us a lesson. Because, we are going the wrong way in politics and in society."

These attitudes should not be overestimated and they also did not appear very frequently in the Soviet media. At that time, the Soviet journalists reported very dramatically, but also very objectively. On the one hand, the bad consequences for the population were always taken into account. On the other hand, of course, reference was also made to the truly heroic missions of the workers who risked or even sacrificed their lives at the scene of the catastrophe, in order to bring the whole thing under control. We still do not know today what is happening in this inner core.

The protective cover that was built over the reactor is quite fragile, which is why a new one is now being placed over it. The entire nuclear power station was only shut down later after some back and forth, because three months after the disaster, reactor unit 3, the adjacent unit, had been put back into operation. It was said that they simply needed the energy. In the meantime, the whole area has been transformed into something else, something that is almost macabre: Ukraine has now designated it as a tourist attraction. There are these so-called adventure tourists who still like to walk around there with gas masks and protective clothing and photograph each other – and pay money for it.

Moderator: Was the fact that shortly after the disaster the 1st of May took place with its public parades etc. one reason for playing down the disaster? Did one simply want to celebrate this day peacefully and not let panic arise?

Grotzky: That was indeed the most important day of the year in the Soviet Union besides the Day of the Revolution. The First of May was and is the people's holiday par excellence and they certainly didn't want to ruin it. After all, in Kiev there were May Parades in public on the street without any protective devices. And we correspondents were also shown the television broadcasts of these parades: "Look! Everything is all right!"

Until about May 9th, the whole thing was still being glossed over by Soviet officials. We, on the other hand, were worried because we had other information from abroad. As a result, our Western ambassadors in Moscow had to react. Therefore, we correspondents turned toward our embassies for information. The British ambassador immediately said: "We send food to the Soviet Union from the West so that our British nationals don't have to eat the possibly contaminated food in Moscow". We all lived in Moscow, less than 435 miles as the crow flies from Chernobyl.

At that time, my family lived in Moscow near the Kiev railroad station and therefore we knew how much food from the Ukraine arrived there every day for the markets in Moscow. Of course, I also wondered what we could do. I had three small children and first of all I sent my wife, an American, and the children to the USA for several months, because I didn't want to take that risk. We then got Geiger counters through the German embassy, because we could not have brought such devices to the Soviet Union through normal customs. Many of us, the American and British colleagues and so on, went from time to time to the markets with Geiger counters and tested the food before we bought it. We discovered that, according to the Geiger counters, some foodstuffs were contaminated. This was shocking to us.

There were also newsletters from the Western embassies telling us all not to get excited. I still have some of these newsletters at home. Reading it today is still frightening. They say that we shouldn't worry about the water in Moscow, because the water would be filtered so that the radioactivity would be filtered out of the water. When you receive such a newsletter from your own embassy to reassure you, then you know: "O no, they don't know that much about the situation either!" Because, radioactivity cannot be filtered out of the water so easily.

At that time in Moscow we were not as badly off in this respect as other areas in Belarus or Ukraine. The consequences, especially in Belarus, were even worse and more devastating. Something happened in this context then that I still cannot explain to myself. Although areas around

Chernobyl had been evacuated, nothing had been done in the neighboring Belarusian villages. But in this area, for example, there had been a very large fallout with an incredibly high level of radioactivity. The people there were not resettled, only the streets were cleaned. The roofs and the houses were decontaminated from the outside. But the people stayed there. I noticed that myself, because I was on the road once with such people during the process of decontamination. Of course, this cleaning was done for me in a very demonstrative and thorough way: I was in Pripyat and these workers drove ahead of me and decontaminated practically every inch in front of me so that I wouldn't get into any radioactivity. I wasn't allowed to touch anything at all. There was a certain risk, of course, and I got cancer later on, but I don't think it was related to that situation. Nevertheless, you naturally become thoughtful afterwards and ask yourself: "Weren't you too careless after all?"

Moderator: After Chernobyl, at the latest since Fukushima, most people are relatively well informed about nuclear accidents. How would you describe the state of knowledge about nuclear power in the Soviet Union back in 1986?

Grotzky: In the Soviet Union, once again, nuclear energy was not a matter for critical reflection. Not at all! Radioactivity in the true sense was only associated with the bombs on Hiroshima and Nagasaki. It was always said that only the USA ever used nuclear weapons. According to Gorbachev, Chernobyl triggered an argument that he still upholds today, when he says: "Chernobyl has shown us how dramatic it would be if we really used nuclear weapons".

Somehow Gorbachev seems to have had bad luck several times in his political career:

In March 1986 he leads a Party Congress and wants to open the doors for everything. But a few weeks later, the Chernobyl disaster happens. Suddenly, all the openness he wants to achieve collapses. This Party Congress was supposed to be a new beginning. Boris Yeltsin, who was completely unknown at the time in the West, appeared at this congress and said that he had not dared to tell the truth, but now he could tell it – namely the truth about this country and its mismanagement. Heydar (Geydar) Aliyev, the father of today's Azerbaijani President, told us back then in a small circle of correspondents that corruption was everywhere throughout the country; but that, unfortunately, not everything could be brought under control, because corruption was so widespread. In other words, there was so much openness that we were quite astonished. That is why we journalists were so surprised that there was no openness at all in dealing with the Chernobyl disaster when it happened.

There was another set back for Gorbachev. On December 7, 1988 he spoke before the United Nations. There he offered the biggest disarmament proposal the Soviet Union had ever made. On the very same day he put this forward, the earth in the than Soviet Republic of Armenia was shaking and there were more then 24,000 deaths from a massive earthquake. No one talked any more about his disarmament proposal, only about the next Soviet catastrophe. Gorbachev, as he told me later, had the feeling that fate was always somehow against him when he tried to push through important political steps.

Moderator: That sounds understandable. What did you personally think about nuclear power before 1986? Has Chernobyl changed your attitude?

Grotzky: Well, I've always been a little skeptical about nuclear energy as a whole. I wasn't quite sure how controllable it all was. I am not an absolute opponent of nuclear power, but I believe that this should only be done with international control. I personally am therefore opposed to nuclear energy being developed and operated at the national level. But there is competition between various countries. In any case, nuclear energy has been driven forward. Finally, there was the disaster of Fukushima with a meltdown, the worst case scenario.

However, this melt down did not lead to the many deaths in Japan; it was the tsunami that cost so many people their lives. Many experts, including Robert Gale, the man I mentioned earlier who is very concerned with the issues of nuclear energy and fallout, say that Fukushima was comparatively mild, unlike what happened in Chernobyl. Even so, the danger of nuclear energy remains.

Pope John Paul II was the first Pope to make a firm statement on nuclear energy. He said that if there was even the slightest risk that man would not be able to master this technology, then we should let it be. This moved many people, and I believe that we must take it seriously.

However, we humans today afford a great deal of technology that kills people or impairs their health. France continues to supply more of half their energy by nuclear power stations, without similar dramatic incidents having occurred there. On the other hand, we also know what can happen. In the United States, too, it is repeatedly denied that nuclear energy causes damage to health. I am very uncertain about this, but in the end I am more opposed to nuclear energy than in favor of it.

Moderator: Above all, it always comes back to haunt you. In April 2015 there were severe forest fires at Chernobyl, which in turn released or stirred up radioactive particles. It was feared that these would be carried by the wind to populated areas. But in this respect, only warning reports came from Ukraine. How do you read or understand such news on the basis of your experiences at that time, if you hear or read about such things today?

Grotzky: Well, we know that a great deal of the radioactivity that has been deposited everywhere has been passed on: via the food chain; via the livestock, to which I said earlier that the contaminated animals were not slaughtered but mixed with the healthy livestock; via plunderers who took things out of this zone; and via all the people who worked there and who, despite all the attempts at decontamination, also passed on their radiation. In other words, we are basically still living with a time bomb.

The next point is that we still don't really know what's going on inside the reactor core. Nobody can get there either. You can make as many protective covers as you want, but what about the ground if it all continues to penetrate further into the earth instead of upwards? It has always been said that this is not possible because the reactor core has been covered all around once more. But are we so sure? If the first explosion could blow up a reinforced concrete ceiling that allegedly weighed 1,000 tons, other things may well happen in the future. I seriously believe that this is still a time bomb for mankind.

Moderator: Do you think that the present and later consequences are still taboo? Because there are some studies that are not fully recognized and that establish correlations between different types of cancer and the contamination at that time or that also in Germany claim an increased leukemia rate in children who grow up near nuclear power plants. There is a lot of criticism, but this criticism is not recognized because these are allegedly not serious studies.

Grotzky: One only needs to briefly research the Internet to see how strong the polarization is in the area of the health consequences of nuclear energy. So we don't know the solution and the question is how we want to deal with the consequences. As long as there is a residual risk - and I am leaning directly on the statement of John Paul II - that man cannot control, I think we should rather keep our hands off nuclear energy. In any case, the consequences of contamination are terrible, as we can see from photographic documents of the present generation: Even children born today still suffer the consequences. There are simply many deformities among the children from all around this Chernobyl disaster.

Measures were also taken at that time which made me very concerned: I know this from a doctor, who was involved in the following: Women who lived in this environment were not only recommended abortions until the sixth month of pregnancy, they were actually ordered to abort their babies. With this, the attempt was made to save the next generation from these malformations. This, of course, had very tragic consequences for many people. Nevertheless, very many children were born with deformities who are still living somewhere today. Of course these people cannot have children themselves; and we know that the consequences of Chernobyl will accompany the population in this region for at least three generations.

Nowadays in Ukraine they say: "We didn't do that, it's a legacy of the evil Soviet era. The Soviet Union no longer exists and Russia does not take any responsibility for such things today. That's why the world community must now take responsibility for Chernobyl."

And it is indeed the case that the world community is financing this new protective covering and all the security measures at Chernobyl. But the international community has never made it its task to eliminate all the consequential damage to the affected people. For this reason, there are still many today, who feel left alone and who only receive support through private aid organizations. This is the really tragic side of it: that many people still suffer directly from this catastrophe.

POSTSCRIPT

This book is a translation from German using the DeepL translator program under https://www.deepl.com/translator.

I would like to thank Dr. Flavio Carsughi for his technical advice and for correcting the translation of the document on pages 20-25.

The original title of this book is:

TSCHERNOBYL
Die Katastrophe
Zeitgenössische Berichte, Kommentare, Rückblicke.

Books on Demand GmbH
Norderstedt 2018

Editor of the English book edition:
Eleanor Grotzky